George Laurence Gomme

Lectures on the Principles of Local Government

Second Edition

George Laurence Gomme

Lectures on the Principles of Local Government
Second Edition

ISBN/EAN: 9783337312343

Printed in Europe, USA, Canada, Australia, Japan

Cover: Foto ©Suzi / pixelio.de

More available books at **www.hansebooks.com**

LECTURES ON THE PRINCIPLES OF LOCAL GOVERNMENT

DELIVERED AT THE LONDON
SCHOOL OF ECONOMICS
LENT TERM 1897

BY

GEORGE LAURENCE GOMME FSA

STATISTICAL OFFICER OF THE LONDON
COUNTY COUNCIL

AUTHOR OF "MUNICIPAL OFFICES" "LITERATURE OF LOCAL INSTITUTIONS"
"THE VILLAGE COMMUNITY" ETC

WESTMINSTER
ARCHIBALD CONSTABLE AND CO
2 WHITEHALL GARDENS
1897

BUTLER & TANNER,
THE SELWOOD PRINTING WORKS,
FROME, AND LONDON.

INTRODUCTION

THIS series of lectures was designed to set forth, if possible, the lines upon which the principles of local government should be studied. At present, principles of local government are not, in this country, considered at all. There is a vague sort of idea that local government is a good thing for Parliament to occupy itself with, but there is no serious attempt to consider it as a subject which is governed by principles and not by fancy, which should not therefore be left to the sudden energy of Parliaments desiring to be busy with something new.

I cannot, and do not, pretend that my effort is anything more than an effort in the right direction. If it turns out to be that, if it should prove to be useful in directing attention to the subject, and bringing about a general desire to ascertain and formulate the principles of local government, sufficient success will have attended it.

In the limits of a term it has not been possible to discuss all the stages of my arguments so as to show the evidence upon which they are founded; and accordingly it will appear as if the method adopted to set the matter before my hearers were purely and simply the *a priori* method of the analytical jurists.

It would be presumption on my part to adopt such a method. I have no right to speak *ex cathedra* on such a subject. And every step of my argument is in reality built up of a large mass of evidence, which I have been examining, both as a student and as an official, for the past twenty years. I cannot set forth this evidence, but I purpose to give a few notes of its chief heads to help the student in the understanding of the lectures—notes similar in effect to those *viva voce* explanations which were from time to time interlineated during the delivery of the lectures, or which formed the substance of answers to the queries of the students after each lecture.

I practically begin my lectures with a differentiation into two classes of the several kinds of local government found in England at the present day. These two classes are the historical, consisting of counties, boroughs, and parishes, and the legislative, consisting of unions and districts. But in describing them I have called them by terms which leave out of sight their origin in historical or legislative times, and bring into prominence their place, or assumed place, as types of local government; that is, I call them respectively local government properly so-called, and quasi-local government. Now the justification for these terms is, I suggest, fully brought out in the course of the lectures, but it will be useful to state shortly what that justification is.

It is, first, that the historical localities have been formed from the settlement of communities whose bond of cohesion was that of common interests. This, therefore, is a formation whose roots lie as deep as possible in the past, and which, by reason of their unbroken continuance, affect to an enormous degree all subsequent influences upon the community. The county was formed from the ancient tribe; the borough from the ancient township in its most favourable position for development; the township from the community who settled down upon the land in economical independence. Hence the formation of the locality of the county, of the borough, and of the township was not due to legislative action, but to forces which belong to the unconscious stages of development in English institutions. This unconscious stage is connected with the natural sociology of man's life, and it is not too much to suggest that we have in those links a strong claim for asserting that local government contains more of the natural history of man than other parts of modern civilization. And let it be noted how very strong is the position which any element of local government must occupy if it can be identified with a phase of the natural history of man.

Secondly, the justification of the terms of classification of the two kinds of local government arises from the historical localities being, and having always been, used for purposes of local government, sometimes directly, sometimes indirectly in the formation of new localities, such as unions and districts. All the influences of common interest which come from these historical localities are, therefore, brought to bear upon the purposes of local government; or, in other words, there are no cases of local government which are not so intimately connected with the historical localities that they can be said to have attained their present position without the aid of influences belonging to the historical localities.

And in point of fact we find that localities formed for special objects instead of all objects of local government are not only imperfect as localities, but as local government centres, being governed as much by the control exercised by the State Government as by the desires of the locality.

These being the facts of the case, the only question that remains to justify the classification adopted in the lectures is, whether such conditions as these should properly represent local government from the point of view of first principles, or whether the two types should be reduced to one type; whether, in short, there can be a dual system, and, if not, whether local government of the historical type should give way to local government of the legislative type.

The answer to this is found, in the first place, from the history of the county, borough, and township, which is the subject-matter of the second, third, and fourth lectures. Everywhere in this history do we find strength and force, and everywhere is this strength and force identified with the development of the locality of the county, borough, and township, from the communities which originally formed the county, borough, and township; locality and community forming two interlaced elements of local government which appear over and over again in the legal and constitutional history of these three local governments, and which have scarcely yet passed out of ken. Government from this standpoint is local in a sense which no other form of government can be local, in a sense which particularly government by unions and districts cannot be local. The true alternative to such a form of government would be not local government but some form of subordinate State government, which can only be called local by reason of the fact that it administers certain services (on behalf of the State) for defined portions of the country. Whatever kind of government this is, it is not local government. It is a substitute for local government—a substitute which rests upon the functions it is called upon by the State to perform, and not upon the locality for which it performs functions.

It is obvious that here arises the important question as to what the functions of local government should be, and this is discussed in the fifth lecture. This introduces the subject of the conflict between private enterprise and government function, and I have attempted on economical lines to define the principles upon which this conflict should be settled. Private enterprise is an undertaking for the common benefit of a particular class of the community, the capitalist, using the word in no invidious or political sense; government service is an undertaking for the common benefit of the whole community, capitalist and consumer alike. That the first has its legitimate range of exercise no economist can deny, and that this range extends into provinces which cannot be bound by localities, scarcely even by nations, is a truth which is daily becoming more and more evident. But then government services have also a legitimate range, and this has been strongly denied, or has been restricted to the narrowest and most incomplete bounds. By limiting the range of the latter to certain well-defined elemental necessities, in which the whole community are equally interested, it cannot be suggested that too sweeping a demand is made. This is a most important part of the subject, and when once it is fairly settled the battle-ground of economical warfare will have shifted its place, and local government will have passed out of the range of its influence.

This, however, leaves for discussion certain questions as to the locality for which the proper functions of local government are to be exercised. Why should the boundary line stop at a given place, instead of extending all over the country without the intervention of boundary lines ? This is a question discussed in the sixth lecture, where the doctrines of benefit and general utility are examined. The area formed by the common interests of a community dating for centuries back in the past is the true locality within which common benefit from new functions of local government will best operate. They will weld with the functions already in existence for the common benefit, and produce further cement for the binding together of the community. Not that this is a fixed area unalterable by circumstances, for it is found that functions which benefit a locality may develop into functions which benefit a larger locality, or the nation at large, and there is room in the operations of true local

INTRODUCTION

government to allow for this process of development. This process is examined in some detail, and its importance as a principle of local government is pointed out.

Common benefits conferred upon localities involve some form of taxation, and this, so far as it affects the subject-matter of these lectures, is very shortly examined in the seventh lecture. I have there attempted to show that all local taxation is a system of payment for a benefit conferred, and that the area of taxation is the correlative problem to that of the area of local government, both being determined by the doctrine of common benefit. Now the benefits from local government services tend to accrue to the owners of local property, by reason of the fact that such property is the conduit pipe through which each person obtains the benefits of the services, and local taxation, therefore, should, as it did originally, fall not upon the person, but upon the owner.

In this way the principles of local government are found so intimately connected one with another as to suggest that they are traceable to deeper instincts in our life than the legislative experiments of a single mind, however great, a single ministry, however capable. It is certain that I have only just touched the fringe of the subject, and that, I am afraid, with but very scanty success. Still, I am emboldened to hope that all my research and all my experience as a local government official may have produced results which, if not conclusive, will lead to their being made so by others more fitted for the heavy task than I can hope to be. In the meantime I hope to continue these lectures with a view of elaborating many of the more important subjects which have been so briefly surveyed in the present series.

I can scarcely close this introduction without thanking a legal friend for his great kindness in looking through the sheets, and giving me many criticisms of value—criticisms which I have always availed myself of, though without making my lectures what my critic would desire. Mr. Herbert Beadle, of the Statistical Department of the London County Council, has also very kindly assisted me in many ways.

LAURENCE GOMME.

24, Dorset Square, N.W.,
    August, 1897.

ANALYSIS OF CONTENTS

Lecture I

1. Object of the lectures—definition of local government; 2. *Preliminary:* limits of the definition—extensions of the definition—classes of local government—growth of new functions produce new forms of local government—different influences of new functions—relationship of local government to the new forms and the new influences—relationship of local government to Austin's definitions—position of local government owing to absence of proper definitions—position of local government before 1888—primary elements of the subject summarized; 3. *Methods:* historical and analytical—both applicable to the present enquiry; 4. *Definition of local government considered:* the term local—localities properly so-called—product of earliest social development—their early power and influence—their decadence—quasi localities—product of administrative system of central government—poor-law unions—urban and rural districts—districts for special purposes—difference in the meaning of local in these two classes of localities—locality a dominant factor—the term government—the authority governing—an elected body—important features of election—Austin's definition—local authorities independent of the State government—dependent upon practically the same electorate as the representative body of Parliament—importance of this in matters of future development—the sanctions for governing—legal sanctions—dependence upon State justice and police—difference between ancient and modern forms of local government in this respect—municipal sanctions—derived from scientific and economical considerations—put in force before State sanctions are called upon; 5. *Relationship of the two classes of local government:* local government properly so-called has acted as a model for quasi-local government—legislative theories; 6. *Relationship of local government to subordinate State authorities*—State

subordinate authorities—commissions ; 7. *Preliminary definitions*—definitions stated—conclusions therefrom.

LECTURE II

1. *Localities properly so-called :* cover the entire area of England—relationship to each other—distinctions of rank among them—importance attached to ancient boundaries—hundreds and great franchises of no influence on local government ; 2. *Counties :* origin in the shire system—formation of the shires according to historians—formed from the ancient tribes—examples from England—from Scotland—development of tribes into kingdoms—of petty kingdoms into the nation—Professor Maitland on the military shire—relationship of the military shire to the tribal shire—formation of a shire system of polity—brings with it many ancient tribal customs—formation of new shires in later times—geographical history not wholly in favour of tribal origins—constitutional history supports tribal origins—the shire-moot—example of the Isle of Man—example *temp.* Canute—example *temp.* William I.—analysis of these examples—changes in the shire system—evidence of the ancient system in the election of coroner—in the right of outlawry—in the ancient electoral system—continuity of site of meeting-place—continuity as a taxing unit—ancient right of assembling—decline of county government under the justices—restoration of county government by the Act of 1888—the county of London—not properly understood—the registration county—locality the great force in the counties—county and county council—county officers—rank of the county—importance of ancient constitution of the county—the hundred—liability for damage transferred to the county.

LECTURE III

Boroughs under the Act of 1888—three classes showing difference in status—this is of modern growth—origin of the burgh in the township—in the Roman sites—*territorium* of the burgh—the legal view—the question of incorporation—legislation of Richard II.—causes and results—burghal property—process of incorporation—the economical view—Roman sites—English sites—combination of burghs—burghal independence—possible development of city organization—burgessship—burgesses and manorial tenants—comparison with Russia—conditions of burgessship—growth of burghal community—land-owning rights of municipalities—tenement and lands are one holding—ancient examples—charter examples—burghal assembly—Professor Maitland's views—village community the basis of the burghal community—the principle of locality involved in this—evidence of the boundaries—burghs contain the town and townlands—locality, therefore, not derived from charters or other administrative Act—summary of this evidence—importance of locality in the case of burghs—internal divisions of the borough were not parishes—the burghal assembly—example of London—continuity of burghal government—close connection between *territorium* and *communitas*—relationship of the burgh to the county.

Lecture IV

Parish the equivalent of the township—growth of ecclesiastical side of the parish—the locality of the township—evidence from Wiltshire and south-east England—locality not formed for administrative purposes—consists of enough land to make each community independent—the agricultural system which belonged to this community—changes in the township organization—its right to hold property—its break up into manorial, ecclesiastical, and civil units—the manorial element—by-law evidence—functions of the township moot—the vestry meeting—*territorium* and *communitas*—right of the township to tax for common purposes—legal objections considered—identification of the township and parish—parishes which were never townships—parishes under the Act of 1894—ecclesiastical parishes—*Summary:* change in the primitive system chiefly due to economical changes under Edward I.—the common interests which created localities still operate—misuse of local terms.

Lecture V

Functions of local government are next to be considered—elements for discussion are two—localities formed by common interests—modern requirements—doctrine of general utility—proper functions of local government not discussed when State imposes new functions—three schools of thought : *laisser faire*, socialistic, economical—John Stuart Mill's definitions—additional qualifications required—limits to the definition—example of bread supply—communal trading not a function of local government—exceptions: pawnbroking, coal supply, sale of alcoholic liquors—functions of local government and private enterprise—private enterprise not entitled to first claim—examples against this—functions of local government not contested by private enterprise in ancient times—examples from London, Chichester, Liverpool, Gloucester—so-called remunerative services are met by a forgotten form of taxation—right of taxation should reside in the taxpayers—examples of taxation in private hands—water supply, cemeteries, gas, electric light, baths and washhouses, tramways, telephones—cost of these met by taxation direct, indirect, or according to benefit—the relation of the services to taxation—compulsory nature of the service is the crucial point—private capital deals only with profitable matters—examples of the cost of services changing from a system of taxation according to benefit to direct taxation—dust-removal, education—examples of mixed systems of taxation—cemeteries, locomotion, telephones, artificial light, fire insurance—examples of direct taxation—water supply—examples of indirect taxation—markets, docks, navigation — services not undertaken by local government—public economics.

Lecture VI

General utility in relation to benefit—some services not apparently of general utility, such as poor relief—the question examined—beginnings of poor relief as a duty of property—early legislation transferred it to the church as a duty—the effect of this in making the ecclesiastical parish the unit of poor relief—effective legislation, however, showed poor relief to be based upon general utility—the case stated—early examples of the effect of neglect of poor upon property—example of St. James' Westminster, of benefit to property by poor relief—economical evidence—poor relief analysed—economical results—agreement between historical and economical evidence that poor relief is founded on general utility—definition of functions in relation to general utility and benefit—relationship of general utility to locality—area of benefit, area of administration, and area of taxation—difficulties met by the principle of differential rating—the subject examined—differential rating and new areas of local government—the principle of development—development of locality and of services—instances of development of locality—boroughs—county boroughs—London county—parishes—instances of development of services—parish services—county services—case of London—instances of development of local services into national services—

prisons—police—metropolitan police—poor law—services of general utility inure to the benefit of property.

Lecture VII

Taxation in relationship to the general principles of local government—present system of Imperial and local taxation—not correlated—absence of information concerning—principle of taxation is co-sharing of taxpayers—extent of co-sharing of Imperial taxes—of local taxes—complexity of the latter—early system of taxation was according to benefit—example of the poor rate and other rates—local expenditure a benefit to property—the term remunerative—services of local government are remunerative services—examples from early Estate Acts—taxation according to benefit—development of taxation according to co-sharing—co-sharing does not eliminate the principle of benefit—classification of the benefits according to the systems of taxation—benefits accrue to property.

I

DEFINITIONS OF LOCAL GOVERNMENT

IT is the object of these lectures to determine the principles of local government—that is to say, the principles of local government as they appear from the English evidence. I am bound thus to limit the subject which I wish to treat upon, because of the time at my command, and also for the sake of conciseness. But the limit is not altogether an evil, for principles, be it remembered, once properly determined are not altered by geography.

I shall approach the subject solely from the standpoint of a scientific analysis of the phenomena presented; and if occasionally the terminology I am compelled to use embraces expressions which unfortunately are tainted by being included in the vocabulary of modern politics, I wish you to bear in mind that such expressions in these lectures bear their literal or scientific sense only.

Local government is that part of the whole government of a nation or State which is administered by authorities subordinate to the State authority, but elected, independently of control by the State authority, by qualified persons resident, or having property, in certain localities, which localities have been formed by communities having common interests and common history.

Before discussing the terms of this definition I have something to say about the general considerations which it suggests.

This definition does not apply to State government in federation, such as the government of Austria and of Hungary under the Austro-Hungarian Empire, and the government of the different states in the United States Republic and in the Swiss confederation. Fortunately, too, it excludes the question of Home Rule for Ireland. But so far as this definition applies to any portion of a political society—a nation, kingdom, or empire—it presents to us that portion separated off, as it were, from all other portions in respect of those matters of government which are administered by the elected body of representatives for the area. The supreme or State government has no administrative jurisdiction within the local area in respect of the matters administered by the elected representatives of that area; while, on the other hand, the electors of the local representative body may be, and in our own country are, as a matter of fact, in conjunction with the remainder of the electors of the country, electors also of the representative body which forms a part of the State government. Thus each local representative authority derives its being from a *portion* of the same electorate from which the State representative authority derives its being; and all the local representative authorities together derive their being from practically the same electorate from which the State representative authority derives its being.

These are the general qualifications or extensions of the definition of local government, and I have next to point out the special qualifications or extensions. These are due to the legislative activity of the past hundred years. It will be found that legislation has not been favourable to the development of local government, that it has supervened in a harassing sort of way, and has introduced into the governmental system of the country institutions that are not local government and that are not State government, but which have been clothed with some of the attributes of each. This process has been fatal to real development. A tendency towards a local development has been stopped by the attributes of State government, and a tendency towards a State development has been stopped by the attributes of local government.

In one sense I do not think it is going too far to say that local government in its true form is that part of the whole government of the country which has not been surrendered by localities to the State but has ever remained in the hands of the community of persons who originated it. The institutions of Anglo-Saxon and mediæval Britain would entirely sanction this statement, and in more primitive civilizations of the present day, such as those represented by India and by Russia, this view would be absolutely correct. But in England of to-day it is in no sense entirely correct, because of the legislative action I have just alluded to; and in the mind of the jurist it is not even partially correct. He would triumphantly point to the case of the boroughs, the most powerful of local institutions, and claim that the frequent surrender of their charters and the re-grant of them by the sovereign shows that local government in the boroughs is simply a system derived from the State, and he would still further point out that the fateful words of the Municipal Corporations Act of 1835—" so much of all laws, statutes and usages, and so much of all royal and other charters and letters patent now in force as are inconsistent with or contrary to the provisions of this Act shall be repealed and annulled"—confirm his view. He would point to the dispossession of the counties of their ancient powers since the reign of Edward I., and the re-grant of powers by the statute of 1888; and to the dispossession of the townships of their ancient powers, in favour of seigniorial jurisdictions and of bodies created by legislation, and the re-grant of powers to the parish as the successor to the township; and he would claim that this dispossession and re-grant of powers in the case of counties and townships further confirmed his view that local government is derived from the State.

Of course the arguments of the jurists are based upon abstract principles, formulated with a view to legislation rather than with a view of historical development. But local government is both historical and legislative in its origin, and the latter has certainly not destroyed the influence of the former.

For the purpose of distinguishing the two classes of local government which appear thus early in the subject-matter I have to present before you, I shall have to introduce rather ugly terms, and it will be convenient if I formally state what these terms are. The two classes I shall term *Local Government properly-so-called*, and *Quasi-Local Government*. The justification for these terms will, I hope, appear in the final results of these lectures, but I may say at once that they are founded upon the distinctions in origin and development of the local governments which make up each of the two classes—distinctions which will appear often in the course of these lectures.

The legislative activity which has produced this cleavage between different forms of local government was not primarily concerned with local government. It had gradually come to be recognised that new functions of government must from time to time be created to meet the growing requirements of civilized society, and the administration of these new functions had to be delegated to an authority other than the State authority itself. Every year almost has witnessed some law placed upon the Statute Book which marks a new departure in the functions allotted to Government authority. The Education Act of 1870 is the most familiar illustration of this, and the Light Railways Act of 1896 is the latest. These new functions have sometimes been imposed upon authorities directly commissioned by the State; sometimes upon local authorities already existing by custom, or by ancient statute; sometimes, as a matter of special legislation, upon newly created authorities—authorities created at the same time and in the same statute as that which created the functions. These alternative methods of carrying out the new functions of government created from time to time have seldom or ever been determined upon a settled plan or principle, either with reference to the kind of functions to be performed or with reference to the area or locality immediately concerned with them.

I pause for one moment to point out the different

influences which the creation of new functions of government exercises. Some of these new functions will be of a character which governing authorities might strongly desire to possess, which they might separately attempt to obtain the sanction of Parliament in order to possess, or which they might conjointly attempt to obtain the sanction of Parliament in order to possess; and the struggle for possession of these functions might rest between the local or subordinate authority and Parliament, or it might rest between the local or subordinate authority and some private interest which is not a governing authority at all. Again, others of these functions will be of a character which governing authorities would *not* desire to possess, but which Parliament, in the interest of the community at large, might seek to impose upon local or subordinate authorities. While it is obvious, therefore, that these two classes of functions produce two different kinds of influence upon the course of local government, it is also clear that they have caused the problems of local government to enter a wider sphere of inquiry than is represented by the surface views of the subject.

Thus local government does not consist merely of certain established phenomena easy to analyse and classify; but is a complex subject, represented partly by established phenomena and partly by an indeterminate group of functions which have not yet wholly ceased to belong to private interests or have not yet been imposed by the State as local government duties. The functions already established have only attained that position by long-existing custom, and it will be found that they do not differ in kind from the undetermined functions. In the meantime, the growth of new functions of government has called into existence governing authorities other than local governments; so that the government of the country is now carried on partly by the State executive authorities and partly by subordinate authorities, which consist of three different classes—namely, local government, quasi-local government, and State commissioned authorities. I shall have to examine these different classes of subordinate authorities in detail presently, but here I want to impress you with the fact that local government has now become one class of the subordinate authorities which the State utilizes for the purpose of carrying on those functions of government which it determines shall not be carried on by the State itself.

Now when it is remembered that this position of local government, as one of three classes of subordinate authorities, has been brought about by the accidents of modern legislation, which, when measured by the admitted triumphs of local government during a period stretching certainly as far back as the

Norman Conquest, must be considered singularly deficient in the capacity for producing any kind of triumph in the art of government, it must be conceded that the position of local government is not satisfactory. The fact is that its development along natural lines has been arrested by a legislative force whose effect is out of all proportion to its ascertained merits. While these merits are at present an unknown factor, the merits of local government are stamped on the constitutional history of the country, and are exhibited in the almost passionate adhesion to the terms and forms of local government in cases where the spirit and reality of it are entirely wanting.

There is one other observation to make at this stage. The fact that local government takes rank among the subordinate authorities of the country brings it into touch with those definitions of government which the lectures of John Austin nearly seventy years ago brought to such remarkable maturity. This great jurist made the first principles of government by a sovereign authority known to all the trained thinkers of the nation, and not the least among the beneficial results of this knowledge was the abolition of all those bitter and lengthy controversies on the principles of government which are associated with the phrases "law of nature," "original contract," "passive obedience," "patriarchal authority," "divine right of kings," etc., which were flung about so disastrously during the eighteenth century. But the principles of government by authorities not dependent upon Parliament or the Crown, but which are, nevertheless, entrusted by Parliament and the Crown with certain functions of government, were never enquired into by John Austin and his successors, and have never been enquired into and determined up to the present time.

Disastrous as was the position of Parliament and the Crown before the scientific definition of government, the position of local authorities, owing to the want of a proper and recognised definition of local government, is still worse. They are not only the sport of "the multitude," but they are the sport of Parliament. All sorts of unqualified persons rush in and make proposals for the settlement of some local government matter with the magnificent irresponsibility which is born of ignorance. Of course many of these proposals kill themselves by their own inherent folly, but many live for a time, and some live on for years. But all, whether they die quickly or live to maturity, serve to distract the public mind from settling down to a system, serve to make busy people devote their energies to the destruction or the defence of first principles, instead of to the application of first principles to new facts, serve to make all local government in some minds a by-word and sport, instead of a matter of very serious import. If any one of you would take the trouble to collect the many schemes which have been suggested during the past forty years relative to the government of London, you will not only illustrate my point most successfully, but you will prove how mischievous it is for these important subjects to remain unsettled. Those of you who may have, or have already had, occasion to consult the local taxation accounts published by the Local Government Board will have a still better opportunity of testing my statement, for it is a startling fact that in no single case—not in London, not in any of the great boroughs, nor in any of the small ones, not in any of the newly created districts, nor even in a single parish, or a single county—is it possible to ascertain, even by minute examination, the local taxation receipts, expenditure or debt of a rating area. The accounts are analysed, not from the point of view of local taxation, but from that of imperial accounting; they are grouped, not according to locality, the basis of all local taxation, but according to the administrative authority—in short, there is nothing but the title to identify them with local taxation.

This was the general position of things before the Acts of 1888 and 1894, and these Acts have rendered it possible to make an attempt towards settlement of principles. It would not have been possible before

1888—at least, not without first performing a task which could not have come within the compass of the lecture room. There then existed localities (county and parish) without government, or without suitable or applicable government, and there existed government (highway authorities, lighting authorities, drainage boards, and the like) without localities, or without localities of a definite characteristic. With incongruities and inconsistencies such as these marking the very starting-point, it is not surprising that they should be accompanied by other incongruities and inconsistencies at every stage. Indeed, it is almost inconceivable into what an inextricable maze the so-called local government system of England had got. Let me try to give an idea of what I mean by means of a few statistics. While the localities to be governed were 15,039 in number, the governing authorities for these localities were as follows :—

Parish Vestries	14,684
Guardians of Poor Law Unions and Parishes	648
Municipal Authorities	303
County Authorities	52
Highway Authorities	6,849
School Boards	2,296
Urban Sanitary Authorities	723
Rural Sanitary Authorities, independently of the Guardians who acted as such	74
Burial Boards	908
Lighting and Watching Inspectors	174
Vestries and District Boards of London	42

Commissioners of Sewers	51
Drainage and Conservancy Boards	230
Fishery Boards	60
Harbour Pier and Dock Trusts	88
Joint Boards	41
Port Sanitary Authorities	57
Commissioners of Baths	28
Library Commissioners	29
Conservators of Commons	4
Market Commissioners	4
Bridge and Ferry Trustees	16

In all some 27,000 different governing authorities, having conflicting jurisdictions, conflicting areas, and all the expensive luxuries of separate and independent life. The Act of 1894 abolished nearly 8,000 of these redundant authorities, and once again introduced the element of locality into local government; the fiat of the Local Government Board in 1896 promised to add to their number by creating a new special authority for pauper children; the policy of the Government in reference to the London water question promises to make a further addition, by ignoring the locality of London in favour of an area formed accidentally by the legislative movements of water supply.

Thus, then, we have as primary elements of the subject to be treated of in these lectures one or two definite facts—namely, the carrying on of a part of the government of the country by authorities subordinate to the State government; the division of these subordinate authorities into authorities dependent upon the State and authorities not dependent upon the State; the position of local government as the origin and chief constituent of authorities not dependent upon the State; the indefinite position which local government thus holds in the national system, and the anomalous results which have arisen by the indiscriminate creation of new authorities for the administration of new functions.

So much, then, for preliminaries.

I must next trouble you with one word as to methods. There are two separate methods of arriving at the final results to be determined—namely, the historical and the analytical. The historical method will show how it was that certain well-defined parts of the kingdom have grown up as units of government, and how certain well-defined functions of government have been carried on by the community composing these units. The analytical method will show, first, that history, having presented to us certain well-defined localities with certain well-defined functions of government, has now altogether ceased to contribute to the elucidation of the principles of local government; and, secondly, that the necessities of the community compel us to turn back from history, or from what has been allowed to grow up with the centuries, to utility, or what should be for the benefit and happiness of the greatest number. Both methods, therefore, are necessary to our purpose, and both methods will be used each in its respective sphere.

I am now ready to go back to the definition of local government with which I commenced this lecture. I shall consider this definition, first, with reference to the meaning and scope of the term *local*, locality; secondly, with reference to the meaning and scope of the term *government*, including therein the connected terms *authority* and *sanctions* for authority.

First, then, with reference to the term *local*. The localities of local government are primarily of two classes: local, properly so-called, consisting of counties, boroughs, and parishes; and quasi-local, consisting of poor-law unions, urban and rural districts, and districts carved out arbitrarily for special purposes.

Of these, the localities properly so-called, in the sense appertaining to local government (that is, the county, the borough, and the parish), are the oldest local units of the country. By this I do not mean that there is any special antiquity about the names county, borough, and parish, but that the localities (apart from the name) which are now known as counties, boroughs, and parishes are of almost unknown antiquity. They are not the creation of an Act of Parliament; they are not, or rather the oldest examples are not, the creation of the sovereign monarch by charter or other instrument of royal prerogative; they are in a sense older than the State itself. Act of

Parliament and charter have, in the course of the long period during which counties, boroughs, and parishes have existed, altered the area of the localities, altered the constitution of the governing authority of the localities, added new counties and new boroughs modelled upon the old examples, but throughout all changes counties, boroughs, and parishes have never ceased to appear upon the map of England as localities which share independently in the government of the country. The influence of these localities has been great in the land. They have always been ready to hand for the use of the State government, whenever emergency or occasion has arisen, and their prescriptive and traditional existence has ever been able to resist serious innovation upon their boundaries. Their powers of government within their own areas began by being rights and privileges which did not exist generally throughout the land, and the rights and privileges often obtaining by virtue of custom and tradition have served to stamp the localities in a special sense as indestructible parts of the kingdom. When King William I., as a conqueror to the conquered, granted to London, "that ye be all lawworthy that were in King Edward's day; and I will that every child be his father's heir after his father's day, and I will not endure that any man offer any wrong to you," and when Exeter claimed the position of an almost independent state, and would only acknowledge William as Emperor of Britain, not as their immediate king or over-lord, the great conqueror was dealing with localities which had not yet come under the Norman principle of government, and which were helping to form the principles which we are at this distant date considering. Local government, therefore, is not in its inception the result of the considered determination of the wise or of the schools and philosophers, but is the result of an unconscious social development; and it comes to this age sanctioned by the combined forces of tradition and sentiment, rather than of reason. No doubt reason and necessity have entered into the considerations which have allowed the continuation of the traditional forms of local government, but reason and necessity have never consciously dominated the forces which have kept up local government. The Norman nobility who arose from the conflict against the West Saxon army at Hastings were covetous of extensive estates and hereditary jurisdictions, the possession of which in the long run crippled the ancient power of the king and the system of local government which existed among the people. Then followed the struggle between the Crown and the Barons, which had the effect in turn of compelling the kings to foster every remnant of local independence amongst the English, as a check on the rebellious and tyrannical policy of the great feudatories (Stubbs, *Historical Documents*, p. 76). Then came the rise of the Commons House of Parliament, who regarded with jealous consideration the existence of jurisdictions outside the scope of the State administration, and who, up to 1888, arranged for the carrying out of the gradually increasing body of new functions of government by almost every possible device except that of local government, and to which we owe that pernicious system of creating a fresh authority for almost every separate function newly created—a system mischievous in its conception, though largely due to the influence of Jeremy Bentham, and mischievous in its results, though it includes within it the system of public elementary education by school boards.

I next turn to the quasi-localities. These are poor-law unions, county districts, and districts for special purposes. The history of the poor-law unions shows how very slightly locality has entered into the considerations which have determined their government; it has not been the common interests of a locality, but the administrative interests of the poor-law system as viewed by the central government department, which has determined the government of the unions; and therefore they appear on the map out of gear with all the other localities, as if superimposed by a people wholly different in race and political instincts from those who had formed the municipal areas. First of all, the so-called Gilbert's Act of 1782 empowered adjacent parishes to unite for poor-law purposes, and sixty-seven unions were thus formed. Then the Act of 1834 gave power to a central board to divide the whole country into districts. The net result of all this legislation is that in England the poor-law system is not really a local system.

The county districts (urban and rural) in their origin do not much differ from the poor-law union, but they have been more fortunate in their history. Formed for the purpose of carrying out the general sanitary laws, they were carved out upon no principle which depended upon the common interests of a locality. They were made out of divided parishes, out of parishes joined together, out of bits of parishes joined to bits of other parishes; they freely cut county boundaries, although generally they were made to conform to poor-law boundaries. Called into being for the purpose of fixing a boundary within which laws applicable to the whole country were to be administered, they were determined by the principle of a central governing authority. The Act of 1894 has, however, done much for them. It gave them a definite relationship to the county and to the county authority, and their future development is likely to conform to the principles of local government.

Districts for special purposes are not based upon considerations of local government at all. Thus the Metropolitan Police District is administered from the Home Office, with the views of the Home Office dominating the whole, and with the result, if I mistake not, that London and the associated areas are paying partly for a national police force and partly for a local force. Other districts are formed for purposes such as drainage, river conservancy and the like, the basis being, not the common interests of a locality, but the administrative interests of a particular service.

It will have been gathered, then, that these districts are local, in the sense applicable to local government, in a manner entirely different from that in which counties, boroughs, and parishes are local. Locality in their case was not the cause but the result of the granting of governing functions. In the one case, locality, being fixed and permanent, and possessing already considerable powers of self-government, is the force at work to attract new functions of government to it, as new functions are created; in the other case, locality has no force at all, and is only created for the purpose of forming a boundary line within which certain new and limited functions of government may be administered. These functions are in the main those that must be administered uniformly throughout the country The limits of choice are very few. Poor-law authorities for instance, may decide to develop their indoor or outdoor system of poor relief, but, whichever system is adopted, the relief of the poor is the one object attained and attainable.

With district councils the latitude is wider. They may decide to control their own water supply; they may administer other optional Acts; but their main duty, the public health Acts, is designed to be administered upon a uniform basis.

Locality, then, is the dominant factor of local government. It is the force which has made counties, boroughs, and parishes remain in undisturbed possession of the most important and the most elementary feature of government—namely, freedom from central control; and which has kept them intact geographically during all the centuries which have witnessed attacks by the Crown, by the feudal nobles, by the modern nobility, and by Parliament. It is the force which lies at the back of the promised system of decentralization of parliamentary functions, which is so often spoken of as one of the necessities of modern times. It is the force which to a large extent determines the character of the governing authority, and differentiates the forms of local government into the two classes which have just been examined.

I have so far discussed the definition of local government with special reference to the term *local*. I must now draw your attention to the definition of local government with reference to the term *government*. There is to consider, first, the authority governing; secondly, the sanctions for governing.

The authority governing a locality in the sense of local government is a body elected by qualified persons living or holding property within the bounds of such locality. The electorate, therefore, is really the governing authority, the elected members being the body to whom, for a certain period, the larger body of electors has delegated its governing powers. The important point about this feature of local government is that the governing body is in no sense appointed or directed by the State government, and I draw special attention to it because in the only passage where John Austin has touched upon this branch of government he uses language which appears to me to be singularly unsuitable. Reviewing "the status or conditions of subordinate political superiors," he includes among the classes bearing political conditions the following:—" 4. Persons commissioned by the State to instruct its subjects in religion, science, or art. 5. Persons commissioned by the State to minister to the relief of calamity—*e.g.*, overseers of the poor. 6. Persons commissioned by the State to construct or uphold works which require, or are thought to require, its special attention and interference—*e.g.*, roads, canals, aqueducts, sewers, embankments."

I am not anxious to dwell upon the limitations of this classification of subordinate authorities in the sense of local government, because they are partly due to the date when Austin wrote and partly to the fact that he did not live to complete his outline. What I do want to dispose of is the phrase "commissioned by the State." Local authorities are not commissioned by the State. They are elected by their own constituencies, independently of State control; they perform the functions of government which belong to them almost entirely in their own way and entirely at their own cost. I am aware, of course, of the limitations which may be advanced against this way of stating the position of local government—the supervisory powers of State departments in some matters of local administration, the grants from Imperial taxation towards the cost of some local services, supply the chief of these limitations. But these are concerned chiefly with the new functions and the new authorities created by legislation; that is to say, they belong to the element of quasi-local government, the functions of which are more often subject to control by the State than they are free from such control.

Indeed, it is not an exaggeration of terms to assert that local government possesses an enormous strength in its ancient derivative force as a representative authority—a force which is in these days sufficiently strong to endow it with just so much power as the electorate choose to demand in real earnest. All such demands are far less jealously regarded than similar demands on behalf of subordinate authorities commissioned or deputed by the State. In a sense I do not see how the elected representatives of the nation would deny to the elected representatives of the whole number of self-governed localities any powers strongly and persistently demanded, for the electorates in each case are practically identical. And it is only a question of the moment as to what powers might be denied to any one or more localities which were not desired by other localities.

The second part of the consideration of the term *government* in the definition of local government has reference to the sanctions for governing. According to the legal classes into which such sanctions fall, they are four in number. They are (1) a considerable code of customary law, not contained in charter or Act of Parliament; (2) Positive law of a general character, or positive law which applies to all localities alike— such, for instance, as the public health Acts; (3) Positive law of a particular character, or positive law which applies to a locality, if that locality chooses to put it into force—such, for instance, as the so-called adoptive Acts relating to free public libraries, etc.; or, again, positive law which applies to only one locality— as, for instance, the many private Acts obtained by localities in almost every session of Parliament; and (4) By-laws enacted by the local authority for the good government of the locality, and being in form an Act of legislation.

It would be idle to deny that these sanctions, different as they are in legal classification, different as they are in origin, do not now depend upon State justice and police for their ultimate force; and herein lies the fundamental difference between ancient and modern forms of local government. Let me draw the picture for you partly from the pages of Mrs. Green's admirable book on *Town Life in the Fifteenth Century.* In the early days the inhabitants of the municipal towns defended their own territory, built and maintained their walls and towers, and held reviews of their forces at appointed times; they elected their own rulers and officials in whatever way they themselves chose to adopt, and distributed among officers and councillors just such powers of legislation and administration as seemed good in their eyes; they drew up formal constitutions for the government of the community, and made, and remade, and revised again their ordinances; no alien officer of any kind save only the judges of the high court might cross the limit of their liberties; the sheriff of the shire, the bailiff of the hundred, the king's tax-gatherer or sergeant-at-arms were alike shut out; the townsfolk themselves assessed their own taxes, levied them in their own way and paid them through their own officers; they claimed broad rights of justice; criminals were brought before the mayor's court, and the town prison, with its iron and its cage, the gallows at the gate or on the town common, testified to an authority which ended only with death; in matters that nearly concerned them they possessed the right to legislate for themselves, and when they were not allowed to make the law, they at least secured the exclusive right of administering it (i. pp. 1–4).

Now, however, this is changed. Whether the State authority exercises wholly new functions unknown to the Middle Ages, or takes over to itself powers which once belonged to local authorities, and makes them serve national, instead of local, ends; whether it asserts a new direction and control over municipal administration, or whether, instead of replacing local authorities by its own rule, it upholds them with the support of its vast resources and boundless strength, every townsman, every burgher, every shireman feels that the State Government, which he helps to constitute by his vote, is charged with the final sanctions for all government (*cf. ibid.*, pp. 124–125). But there is still a great force, moral if not legal, sentimental if not constitutional, in what may be termed the intermediate sanctions of municipal custom and municipal rule. I am compelled to say municipal here, because in the towns and in the counties the great sanctions of local government have been stifled out, though not, I hope, for so long a time as to be incapable of being revived by the new life which is now opened out to them. These sanctions are derived from all that is best in our natures—from the love that we bear to our birthplace, to our place of up-bringing, to the familiar scenes of our playing-time and our work-time, of our griefs, misfortunes, and cares, of our successes and good fortune—to our fondness for being classed as Kentish men, as Dorsetshire men, or even as Londoners. They are derived, too, from the demands of science, which have laid bare some of the first necessities of health and of life, particularly in places with crowded populations, and which are found to be necessities only to be met by common action. Finally, these sanctions are derived from economical considerations. Strong and powerful, therefore, as are the sanctions for local government derived from the State law and State police, the sanctions proceeding directly from local government itself are as strong. Because they are put in motion constantly, and because they operate quietly and upon great masses of people, they are not so much in evidence as the State sanctions, which are only put in motion when the municipal sanctions have failed; but, if I mistake not, it is the constant action and wide operation of these sanctions of local government which are the real cause of the new departure in modern legislation relating to local government matters.

Looking back upon the distinction which I have drawn between the two classes of local governments, it will be seen that while in the matter of locality the local governments properly-so-called and the quasi-local governments were not on the same footing, in the matter of representative governing authority they are quite on a par. This, indeed, is the real force which has given quasi-local government its vitality. The election of a representative authority, even if its powers are limited to the administration of certain fixed duties, is a force which tells for good. When that force is combined with the force which is derived from a locality fostered under the influence of common interests of long-continued standing, or of strong, immediate character, the tendency is towards local government of the true type,—county, borough, or parish; and it is to these combined forces that we owe the growth of the modern municipal borough, and, in the case of London, of the modern county—a growth that will compel us to consider a great principle of local government later on: namely, the principle of development. One other point will have become clear to you: namely, that localities properly-so-called have, in a sort of unconscious fashion, served as models for the purpose of extending the machinery of government by authorities subordinate to the State, and hence the *idea* of local government has become a fixed point in the national will. It is from this *idea* that has proceeded so much of the political talk about local government, and so much of the credit allotted to England as the mother-home of local government. But in being satisfied with the idea much of the substance has not been obtained. Indeed, the very looseness with which the models have been copied testifies to the fact that localities have never been allowed to develop their own system of government in a natural way, in the same manner as they developed down to the end of the Middle Ages. Everything is now governed, not by the needs of the locality, but by the cast-iron mould of legislation, which allows no room for even some of the elementary difficulties, and certainly not for the greater difficulties attending the growth and expansion of localities from the condition of a simple parish to that of a borough, or of a group of parishes to that of a county.

If I have succeeded in fixing attention upon the primary elements of local government, and if, further, I have shown that the growing functions of government which must be delegated by the State affect very largely the future of local government, there is still another part of the subject which must be dealt with in this preliminary survey—namely, the position which local government holds in reference to the other subordinate authorities of the State. Let me remind you that local government derives its power from, and is answerable to, the electors—a portion of the whole body of electors who form the representative element of the State government; and that the other subordinate authorities derive their power from, and are answerable directly to, the State government.

Now we have already seen that local government in modern times practically forms two out of three classes of subordinate authorities which it has become necessary for the State to use or to create for the purposes of carrying on the affairs of the country. In order to understand the position of local government in relation to the State, apart from local government itself, it is necessary to give a very short account of that third class of subordinate authorities which are not wholly devoted to local affairs. I am obliged to say "not wholly devoted," because it will be found that they include one kind of authority which performs functions of strictly local government.

This class of subordinate authorities consists of (1) the judges and other ministers of justice; (2) central departments of State, like the Board of Trade, Local Government Board, Patent Office, and other sections of the Civil Service; (3) commissions appointed by the State government, and responsible to the State government. The two first of these subordinate authorities need not concern us more than is sufficient to take note of their constitution in relation to the State. But commissions appointed by the State closely touch the subject of local government. Up to the year 1888 the counties were entirely in the hands of such commissions; there are a few of them left elsewhere who perform functions generally performed by local governments. These were created for some special purposes of drainage, fisheries, docks, river conservancy, and the like, and, in the case of the Home Counties and London, of police. They possess in most cases powers of taxation, direct or indirect, and they are not responsible to the locality which is taxed, but only to the State. Standing in direct contrast to local government, locality is no real or essential element in their constitution or their responsibilities. What they have to do with is a section of the kingdom, not a locality. The duties they have to perform are not for the locality, but for the State. The contrast is, of course, a vital one, though I think it is but little understood.

We can now, I think, venture upon a preliminary classification and definition of the elements of government with which we have to deal for the purpose of determining the principles of local government. That, on the one hand, we have found local government in a sense the basis of a system of quasi-local government, and, on the other hand, in a sort of conflict with commissioned or deputed government, shows clearly enough that local government is not of itself a simple element, but part of a larger, complex subject, to the divisions of which it stands in definite relationship. I shall not at this stage be able to attempt definitions which will answer to all the requirements; but those elements which have been brought into prominence in this lecture provide sufficient material for the practical working purposes of making the subject clear as far as we have hitherto proceeded.

The elements of government which thus occur for classification and definition are as follows :—

1. The State has allowed for many centuries, and still allows, certain localities within the national area to be governed, in all but State matters, by elected representative authorities.

2. These localities are counties, boroughs, and parishes, and cover between them the entire area of the kingdom.

3. The functions of government exercised by these localities are not all confined to independent areas; thus the councils of the counties exercise functions within some boroughs and within all parishes; the borough councils exercise functions within parishes.

4. The State has created from time to time new functions of government, and is still continuing to create new functions.

5. The State has imposed these new functions on county councils, on borough councils and on authorities created for the special purpose for an area of a quasi-local character.

6. The characteristic of these newly created functions of government is that they must be administered upon a common plan or standard all over the king-

dom, or the neglect of one locality may become an injury to the nation; those functions which do not come under this definition are generally specifically optional in their character.

7. The cost of administration is met by the taxpayers, direct or indirect, of the locality for which the functions of government are carried out.

8. Certain functions of government generally exercised by self-governed localities are in some cases exercised by commissions appointed by the State.

9. Certain supervisory and legislative functions of local government are exercised by departments of the State—the Local Government Board and the Board of Trade.

10. Other functions of government are exercised by subordinate authorities of the State for State purposes only, and having no relationship to local government.

These definitions, I think, contain the chief elements of the subject as they appear from the analysis attempted in this lecture. The particular value of each element in determining the principles of local government does not appear here, but will, I hope, be made evident as I proceed with the subject, but the order in which I have, by the logic of the case, placed these different elements is a matter for consideration at this point.

The localities which have been self-governed from

the earliest times of our constitutional history, or which have been granted self-government on the same principle, as the earliest cases stand first among the subordinate authorities of the State; while the localities created to serve special purposes have no place until after the element of new functions of government has been brought into being. The problems of local government hinge round these two classes of institutions, and the lectures to which I shall have to ask your attention will be devoted to settling, or attempting to settle, some of the questions which arise out of these problems. Such questions are not idle academics. They are the questions, or some of the questions, which have failed to be answered hitherto on occasions when the demand for answers has been of a singularly urgent nature. London, for instance, put these questions in 1855, and at several periods since then have these selfsame questions been put on behalf of the capital of the empire. Partly answered in 1888, they are being put again in the present day with all the passion of conflicting parties. It is, however, not amidst conflict that such questions can be answered. The appeal is to the analytical inquirer, and the subject-matter is the principles of local government as determined in history and by the doctrines of general utility.

II

LOCALITIES—COUNTIES

WE have, as I showed in my first lecture, to start with the existence of localities, properly so-called. If I had been following strictly the analytical method of inquiry, it would doubtless have been necessary to first determine what the functions of local government are, or may be; and then to have determined what the form, powers, and constitution of the local authority are, or may be. But I do not reject the lessons of historical development, and I hold that it is not only logical, but essential to begin with the facts of history, and to proceed from these to the conclusions to be based on the doctrine of general utility.

The localities, properly-so-called, have been already named as counties, boroughs, and parishes, and it is important to bear in mind that between them they cover the entire area of England and Wales; or, to put it in another way, the entire area of England and Wales contains within it a certain number of localities, properly-so-called, and there is no part of this area left outside these localities. I hope you notice that I do not say that England is *divided* into localities properly-so-called, but that it *contains* them. And the significance of this distinction lies in the fact that the aggregation of these localities has made the kingdom, and not that the kingdom, having been formed by political forces, was then divided up into sections for administrative or other purposes.

This statement, however, needs explanation. The entire area of England and Wales is allotted to counties, and also to parishes, counties and parishes thus occupying the same area. But there are only certain selected areas which are boroughs, and these areas are also divided into parishes. The boroughs are of two kinds—county boroughs and non-county boroughs. Within the area of the former the county authorities have (with some exceptions) no jurisdiction; within the area of the latter they have a limited jurisdiction. Therefore we may put this question of areas into the form of an equation, with the following result :—

(1) Counties + county boroughs = the whole country.
(2) Parishes = the whole country.
(3) Non-county boroughs + parishes
     in the counties = the whole country.

It will be seen that the localities grouped in these three different ways comprise between them, in each grouping, the entire area of the country; and they must, therefore, bear a certain relationship to each other. The relationship of county to county borough is one of mutual independence, except that the county has, in some formal matters and in some special exceptions, a jurisdiction within the county borough. The relationship of county to parish, and to some extent of county borough to parish, is that of an entity to its constituent parts. The extent to which the county boroughs conform to this relationship is measured by the extent to which they have spread beyond their ancient municipal boundaries. In thus extending their areas they have taken in either whole parishes or parts of parishes from the county, and thus the included parish boundary makes the limit of the new county borough boundary. In the cases where the county borough has not extended its boundary into the county, its municipal boundary is determined, not by parishes, but by the same considerations as those which govern ordinary municipal boroughs—considerations, namely, of common interest, which caused communities in early times to settle down upon and utilize certain tracts of territory; and in these cases the relationship of the county borough to the parish is the same as that of the municipal borough to the parish. The relationship of the municipal borough to the parish is, in all ancient boroughs, that of an area divided into smaller areas for purposes other than municipal purposes—namely, for purely ecclesiastical purposes. These points are somewhat technical, and I am not at all sure I have made them understood, but the point I wish to bring out is that, though counties, county boroughs, and municipal boroughs, are all equally areas containing smaller areas known as parishes, the parishes contained in counties, and to are limited extent already noted in county boroughs, are constituent parts of the counties or county boroughs, while the parishes contained in municipal boroughs are artificial divisions which do not rank as constituent parts. I shall have to examine this position somewhat more narrowly later on, but here it is important as establishing a distinction of an elemental character between the relationship of counties to parishes and the relationship of boroughs to parishes.

I am anxious to show you that there are certain distinctions of rank among the localities we are now considering—distinctions which have to some extent lost their force in the unmeaning talk of political parties, but which, nevertheless, have descended with the localities from ancient times, and could be made exceedingly important in meeting the necessities of modern times. To some extent, indeed, this distinction in rank is being recognised already. Thus the units which are made by the Act of 1888 the recipients of grants from Imperial taxation to local taxation are the counties and county boroughs; and the share of the lesser units in these grants (the municipal boroughs, the district councils, and the poor-law unions) is obtained from the amounts first allotted to counties and county boroughs. Again, certain administrative functions in connection with the lesser units are placed in the hands of the counties and county boroughs, both by the Acts of 1888 and 1894, and the trend of events in educational legislation is distinctly in the same direction.

Thus, both historically and in modern practice, there are degrees of rank among these localities. The county takes the place of the highest unit of government, next in rank to that of the State or kingdom itself; the county borough practically ranges itself alongside of the county, though still in a very few matters of formal functions, such as belong to the Lord Lieutenancy, it is subordinate to the county; the municipal borough comes next in rank to the county borough, with a tendency and a constitutional capacity to be promoted to the rank of county borough; and the parish comes at the bottom of the system, the lowest unit of government in England and Wales, with a separate gradation of rank according to whether it is the parish of a county or the parish of a municipal borough.

I want next to direct your attention to the importance of the fact that these localities, formed by the almost irrecoverable events of unrecorded history, divide between them the entire area of the country. They have survived all shocks, all revolutions, all changes, and their position on the map of England is as indestructible as the country itself. Even in these days, one of the most difficult operations to perform is to alter a parish, or a borough, or a county boundary. We in London, for instance, prefer to have our county invaded by a district of Middlesex at South Hornsey, and in turn to invade the county of Middlesex with our detached piece of territory at Muswell Hill, and the county of Surrey with the smallest fragment of detached territory at Barnes. We prefer also to see our natural watershed boundary eaten into on the north at Willesden and on the south at Beckenham. Internally, too, all that is left of the ancient city of Westminster prefers to be in two detached parts; Chelsea will not surrender its detached piece at Kensal Green; Kidbrooke detached and Clapham detached are also staunch to their historic boundaries. This kind of thing extends all over the country, and legislation which provided means to get it altered (7 and 8 Vict., cap. 61, and 30 and 31 Vict., cap. 106) has not succeeded.

It is with such material as this that the groundwork of local government in this country is formed. The historic hundred has, alone of all ancient local institutions, dropped out of existence for administrative purposes, and this has left the map of England covered with counties and parishes, dotted here and there with boroughs; each with a long history, each standing to others of the same class on a footing of equality, and to the other classes in definite historic and practical relationship. The great franchises, like the Duchy of Lancaster, the Duchy of Cornwall, and the Palatinate of Durham, have scarcely left their mark upon local government; smaller franchises, like cathedral closes, as at Salisbury, and abbey closes, as at Westminster, and like the Inns of Court of London, are to some extent outside the general local government system, but they conform in many important particulars, and they are units of local government in themselves. There is, indeed, practically no part of the country outside the historic system of local government, no part of the country not contained in a county, a borough, or a parish; no part of the country, therefore, which has not received from its history, in one shape or another, a defined area of common interests—first, in the extended sense of the county; secondly, in the concentrated sense of the borough; thirdly, in the limited sense of the parish. There was room enough here for every measure of reasonable reform, for every allowance for natural development, for a perfect system of local government, with all the added functions of modern times. The principles of local government have their foundation here, and it will be a part of my task in these lectures to trace out how this heritage from the past has been used for later requirements.

What, then, is the origin of these historical units—these localities, properly-so-called—which thus divide between them the entire area of the country? I begin with the county, and I make the preliminary observation that in all cases of appeal to history I shall deal only with that part of the ancient conditions of local government which lead directly to the subject-matter of these lectures—namely, the principles of local government. All the archæological and antiquarian interest of the subject, which is immense, I do not touch upon, but I point out in passing that students would do well to look this part of the subject up for themselves. It is absorbing in its vivid interest, and it would illustrate and redeem much of the unavoidable dryness and technicalities of the subject-matter of these lectures.

The county as a local institution is practically peculiar to Great Britain. In Hungary there is something analogous to it, but it is not the county; and in other countries there are local divisions which approach the English county in its modern aspect, but not in its historical aspect. We must seek for the origin of the county in the far more ancient shire. A great deal has been written about the origin of the shire, including the work of such writers as Bishop Stubbs, Freeman, Kemble, and Palgrave; and it may seem presumptuous if I suggest that these authorities have begun their investigation at the wrong end. They have begun with the township, and endeavoured to build up an aggregate of townships to form the hundred, or higher grouping, and an aggregate of hundreds to form the shire, thus suggesting an artificial origin for the shire, as the deliberate act of a monarch or other sovereign authority, only to be formed after the lesser areas have been formed—only, in fact, an aggregation of so many of the lesser areas. I believe this to be entirely wrong. I think the exact reverse of this process is the true state of things. I think the shires are the remains of the ancient tribal settlements, the tribes dividing themselves out within their territory—the shire—into communities, which afterwards became townships, and, as we shall presently see, parishes. The point is obscure, and would need a long treatise to work out in detail, but I will state shortly the chief facts in support of this view of the case.

We have it on the authority of Bishop Stubbs that the English invaders came into Britain "in the full organization of their tribes" (*Const. Hist.*, i. 64). Mr. Skene's examination of the Scottish tribal system, Sir Henry Maine's of the Irish tribal system, Mr. Seebohm's recent investigation into the tribal system of Wales, and, may I add, my own later investigation into the survivals of tribal religion in all parts of the United Kingdom, show very thoroughly that the tribal organization was a force in early English institutions.

How, then, do we find the tribal organization appearing upon the map of England when the map of England was beginning to be made out by the earliest writers? My first point is that there are a great many territorial divisions called shires, much smaller than the modern shire, and of which I will only recall to your memories Hallamshire, Richmondshire, and Allertonshire in our modern Yorkshire, as the best-known modern survivals. Now these small shires have no constitutional history whatever, and are simply names of territories which did not remain of administrative significance after the formation of the kingdom. On the other hand, there are shire names which appear in the Saxon Chronicle after the time of Alfred as appertaining to our modern shires, but which before the time of Alfred appear as tribal names pure and simple. Thus the Wilsætan [tribe] become Wiltshire, the Eastseaxan become Essex, the Suthseaxan become Sussex, the Middleseaxan become Middlesex; and we also find the Dornseatan of the Anglo-Saxon Chronicle appear as Dorsetshire in Simeon of Durham, and the Sumorzætan as Somersetshire. Thus we have territories called shires which are not the constitutional shires of the country, and we have tribal names developing into the names of the constitutional shires. Further, Norfolk and Suffolk are simply the north and south tribal divisions of the East-Anglian people, while Berkshire, Surrey,

Kent, and Sussex are four of the ancient Saxon kingdoms.

The analogous condition of things in Scotland which Mr. Skene has worked out with such conspicuous success (*Celtic Scotland*, vol. iii.) supplies, at least, evidence for the early history of Teutonic institutions in North Britain, which it does not do to altogether neglect when we are considering from the less perfect materials the possible line of development in South Britain. It must be remembered that there are still districts marked on the map by the name of a people, and not by any government machinery. The Meonwaras of Hampshire gave their tribal name to the hundreds of East and West Meon; the Mægsætas, Mersewaras, Gevissi, Hwiccas, Hecenas, Lindisfaras, Peak settlers, Chiltern settlers, Gyrvians, are all pure tribal names, which, in one way or another, have influenced the modern geography of England.

But between the tribal territorium and the kingdom there lies a whole stage of political development. This development, we cannot doubt, began by certain tribes bringing themselves up to the position of kingdoms. The history of Anglo-Saxon Britain is the history of the evolution of kingdoms out of tribes, and of the three larger kingdoms of Northumbria, Mercia, and Wessex out of the petty kingdoms. Districts that had once been kingdoms could not, under the Anglo-Saxon kingship, have altogether lost their individuality, and thus when the whole country became united under Edgar, that monarch held together a federation of kingdoms and sub-kingdoms, rather than one thoroughly fused kingdom.

At this stage there comes in another point of interest, and which Professor Maitland has recently investigated. "The exceedingly neat and artificial scheme of political geography," he says, "that we find in the Midlands, in the country of the true shires, forcibly suggests deliberate delimitation for military purposes. Each shire is to have its borough in its middle. Each shire takes its name from its borough. We must leave it for others to say in every particular case whether and in what sense the shire is older than the borough, or the borough than the shire; whether an old Roman chester was taken as a centre, or whether the struggles between Germanic tribes had fixed a circumference. But a policy, a plan there has been, and the outcome of it is that the shire maintains the borough" (*Domesday Book and Beyond*, p. 187).

I am afraid Mr. Maitland is not really so ready as he says to leave it to others to decide whether the shire was the outcome of this definite policy and plan or was older than it; and in particular I am afraid he will resist my appeal to primitive tribal history to decide the point. But, fully accepting his brilliant theory of the military relationship of the shire to the borough, according to the policy and plan of Edward the Elder and of Alfred—for Alfred is traditionally said to have divided the kingdom into shires—I see here the definite beginning of a plan distinct from the previous indefinite growth and development of primitive institutions. But the plan had materials to work with. It did not have a clean sheet—a map of England with only its coastline drawn—to work upon. It had its tribal territory, roughly equivalent to the ancient shire territory; it had its boroughs, roughly equivalent to the Teutonic development of the city government, a matter I shall describe in a later lecture ; and from these two materials the genius of Edward and of Alfred met the political difficulty of their day, and formed a shire system of polity, instead of a tribal system.

But a shire system of polity so formed was the means of bringing the primitive tribal system into active operation among the national institutions, and, therefore, of preserving all of its primitive elements which were not immediately required for the new system. It is thus that the shire has become the basis of local distinctions older than the kingdom, as when philologists first turned their attention to the scientific value of dialects in the history of a language they perceived that the ancient shire divisions were also dialect divisions. Language is a great dividing line; but within the boundary formed by such dividing lines it cements people together in a fashion that no Act of Parliament can accomplish.

Of course, the final territorial sub-divisions of the country included the formation of new shires or counties. Thus the shires of Northumbria were established at a very late period, for at the time of Domesday survey Northumberland, Cumberland, Westmorland, and Durham are not described, and other counties are not described under their present boundaries. But these new formations were modelled upon the older self-grown shires, and they do not really form an exception to the origin of the shire in the ancient tribal kingdoms.

I do not suggest that this is the last word to be said upon this important subject, nor that it explains all the difficulties against the tribal origin of the shires; but if we turn from the consideration of their geographical history to some facts in their constitutional history, we shall find further support for the view here taken.

Bishop Stubbs states that "in the shire-moot as a folk-moot, we have a monument of the original independence of the population which it represents" (*Const. Hist.*, i. 116); and I draw attention to the significant fact that there is evidence to show that the independent sanction of the shires was at one time necessary to make valid the laws promulgated by the national council (Elton, *Tenures of Kent*, 38; Stubbs, *Const. Hist.*, i. 115). To these points must be added the evidence as to the ancient meeting-places of the shires

—in the open-air, under a sacred tree, on a hallowed mound, or near a revered monolith; sure indication of the ancient gathering-place of free tribesmen, met to put in force laws and customs which were theirs by inheritance, and not by favour. I have traced out the importance of this feature in a book of mine, published in 1881, *Primitive Folk-moots*, when I first began as an enthusiastic, and I am afraid not very scientific, enquirer into the history of local government. If I now wished to dwell upon the archaic side of things, instead of upon the practical, I could not adduce a better example of the origin of the shire in an independent tribal unit, grown later into a petty kingdom, than the constitutional status of the Isle of Man. It has its own governing authority, meeting to this day formally on the Tynwald Hill, in the open air, and preserving that significant feature of the English shires that no Act of the Imperial legislature is valid in Manx territory until promulgated by the Manx court at the Tynwald Hill. Here, in actual and continuous life, is every feature of the ancient shire as it once was in England. The Manx kingdom has never really come under the crushing power of the English sovereignty; there was no necessity for it, and so it remains stranded among the progressive elements of our constitution, as a survival from, and an example of, the earliest forms. If it were ever thought desirable, and it is not likely, to bring the

Isle of Man into the English system of government, the isle would be constituted a county, and then we should have evidence of the entire process by which the English counties have grown into being.

What the shire-moot was in ancient times may be ascertained from the record of a suit in the reign of Canute. A translation of this has been given by Hallam (*Middle Ages*, p. 508), and I quote it here for reasons that will presently appear. " It is made known by this writing that in the shiregemot held at Agelnothes-stane [Aylston, in Herefordshire] in the reign of Canute there sat Athelstan the bishop, and Ranig the alderman, and Edwin his son, and Leofwin, Wulfig's son ; and Thurkil the White and Tofig came there on the king's business ; and there were Bryning the sheriff, and Athelweard of Frome, and Leofwin of Frome, and Goodric of Stoke, and all the thanes of Herefordshire. Then came to the mote Edwin, son of Enneawne, and sued his mother for some lands, called Weolintun and Cyrdeslea. Then the bishop asked who would answer for the mother. Then answered Thurkil the White, and said he would if he knew the facts, which he did not. Then were seen in the mote three thanes that belonged to Feligly [Fawley, three miles from Aylston], Leofwin of Frome, Ægelwig the Red, and Thinsig Stægthman ; and they went to her and inquired what she had to say about the lands which her son claimed. She said that she had no land which belonged to him, and fell into a noble passion against her son, and calling for Leofleda, her kinswoman, her wife of Thurkil, thus spake to her before them: 'This is Leofleda, my kinswoman, to whom I give my lands, moneys, clothes, and whatever I possess after my life'; and this said, she thus spake to the thanes: 'Behave like thanes, and declare my message to all the good men in the mote, and tell them to whom I have given my lands and all my possessions, and nothing to my son,' and bade them be witnesses to this. And thus they did: rode to the mote, and told all the good men what she had enjoined them. Then Thurkil the White addressed the mote and requested all the thanes to let his wife have the lands which her kinswoman had given her; and thus they did, and Thurkil rode to the church of St. Ethelbert, with the leave and witness of all the people, and had this inserted in a book in the church."

The points of importance to note about this singularly interesting record are as follows:—

(1) The ancient shire-moot was a primary assembly composed of all the thanes of the shire, and not a representative assembly composed of elected members.

(2) That it was held at a great stone in the open air.

(3) That the bishop and alderman sat there of

their own right, and that there were two representatives of the king.

(4) That it adjudicated upon pleas of land.

What the shire-moot was immediately after the Conquest may be gathered from the record of a great meeting of the Kentish shiremen in 1072, at Pennenden Heath, the ancient meeting-place, in the open air, and still the site of the modern meeting-place of the county council, the County Hall at Maidstone. I lay some stress upon this continuity of site for the meeting-place of the county assembly, and there are other points of importance to which I shall direct your attention.

I shall use a translation of the earliest recorded account of the transaction I am about to examine, because there can be no improvement upon the simple terseness of the chronicle language :—

"In the time of the great King William, who conquered the English kingdom and subjected it to his rule, it happened that Odo, Bishop of Bayeux, and the king's brother, came into England much earlier than Archbishop Lanfranc, and resided in the county of Kent, where he possessed great influence and exercised no little power. And because in those days there was no one in that county who could resist a man of such strength, by reason of the great power which he had, he seized many lands belonging to the archbishopric of Canterbury, and some customs, and by usurpation added them to his rule. But it happened not long after this that the aforesaid Lanfranc, Abbot of Caen, also came into England, by the king's command, and, by the grace of God, was raised to the archbishopric of Canterbury, and made primate of all the realm of England. When he had resided there for some little time, and found that many lands anciently belonging to his see were not in his possession, and discovered that, by the negligence of his predecessors, these had been seized and distributed, after diligent inquiry, being well assured of the truth, as speedily as possible, and without delay, he made suit to the king on that account. Therefore the king commanded all the county [*comitatum totum*] to sit without delay, and all the men of the county—Frenchmen, and especially Englishmen learned in the old laws and customs—to assemble. When these were assembled on Pennenden Heath [*apud Pinendenam*], all together deliberated. And when many suits were brought there for the recovery of lands, and disputes about the legal customs were raised between the archbishop and the aforesaid Bishop of Bayeux, and also about the royal customs and those of the archbishop, because these could not be ended on the first day, the whole county [*totus comitatus*] was detained there for three days. In those three days Archbishop Lanfranc recovered many lands which were held by the bishop's men—namely, Herbert, son of Ivo, Turold of Rochester, Ralph de Courbe-Espine, and many others, with all the customs and everything which pertains to those lands—from the Bishop of Bayeux, and from his men above mentioned, and from others —namely, Detlinges, Estokes, Prestetuna, Damtuna, and many other small lands. And from Hugh of Montfort he recovered Rucking and Brook: and from Ralph de Courbe-Espine, pasturage of the value of sixty shillings in Grean [Island]. And all those lands and others he recovered so free and unquestioned that, on that day on which the suit was ended, not a man remained in the whole realm of England who could make any complaint thereof, or bring any claim, however small, to those lands. And in the same suit, he recovered, not only those lands aforesaid and others, but he also revived all the liberties of his Church and all his customs, and established his right in them when revived—soca, saca, toll, team, flymena fyrmthe, grithbrece, foresteal, haimfare, infangentheof—with all their customs, equal to those or smaller, on land and on water, in wood, on road, and in meadow, and in all other things within the city and without, within the burg and without, and in all other places. And it was proved by all those upright and wise men who were there present, and also agreed and judged by the whole county [*toto comitatu*], that, as the king himself holds his lands free and quiet in his domain, the Archbishop of Canterbury holds his lands in all things free and quiet in his domain. At this suit were present Geoffrey, Bishop of Coutances, who represented the king, and held that court; Archbishop Lanfranc, who, as has been said, pleaded and recovered all; also the Earl of Kent—namely, the aforesaid Odo, Bishop of Bayeux; Ernest, Bishop of Rochester; Agelric, Bishop of Chichester, a very old man, and most learned in the laws of the land, who was brought there in a wagon, by the king's command, to discuss and explain the ancient legal customs; Richard of Tunbridge; Hugh of Montfort; William of Arques; Haimo, the sheriff; and many other barons of the king and of the archbishop; and many men of those bishops; and other men of other counties; also men, both French and English, of much and great authority with all that county. In the presence of all these, it was shown, by many most evident proofs, that the King of England has no customs in all the lands of the Church of Canterbury, except three only; and the three which he has are these: First, if any man of the archbishop digs into the king's highway, which runs from city to city; second, if any one cuts down a tree near the king's highway, and lets it fall across the road. Concerning these two customs, those who are taken in the act while so doing, whether pledge may have been received from them or not, yet, at the prosecution of the king's officer and with pledge, shall pay what ought justly to be paid. The third custom is of this kind. If any one on the king's highway sheds blood, or commits homicide, or does any other unlawful thing, if he is seized in the act and detained, he shall pay the fine to the king; but if he be not seized there, and shall once more depart thence without giving pledge, the king can justly exact nothing from him. In like way, it was shown in the same suit that the Archbishop of Canterbury ought to have many customs on all the lands of the king and the earl; for, from that day on which Alleluia is ended to the octave of Easter, if any one sheds blood, he shall pay fine to the archbishop. And at any time, as well in Lent as at any other time, whoever commits that offence which is called cildwite, the archbishop shall have either the whole or the half of the fine— in Lent the whole, and at any other time either the whole or half of the fine. He has also, in all the same lands, whatever seems to pertain to the care and safety of souls."

Now if we analyse this record we have the following facts about the shire-moot of Kent in 1072:—

(1) The dispute was between two Kentish men— Odo, Earl of Kent in this case more than Bishop of Bayeux, and Lanfranc, Archbishop of Canterbury.

(2) The subject-matter of the dispute was the possession of landed property.

(3) The attendance of all the men of the county, especially those learned in the old laws and customs, was required.

(4) The place of meeting was on Pennenden Heath, in the open air.

From these facts it is clear that Kentish questions, in 1072, were decided by Kentish men; that the domain of national law did not then include the customary land laws; that local customs were interpreted by the inhabitants of the district, according to traditional usage; and that the meeting-place was held in the old tribal fashion, and, as the evidence of Domesday shows, on the spot which was sacred to the gathering of the shire-moot of Kent.

It is true that side by side with these most important facts are other facts significant of changes about to happen, rather than of changes which had already happened. These are (1) that the representative of the king, a Frenchman, presided over and held that court; (2) that Agelric, Bishop of Chichester, not a Kentish man, but most learned in the laws of the land, was present, as a sort of assessor; (3) that "other men of other counties" were present. These extra county elements mar the perfection of the picture; but they do not take away the local character of the court and of the proceedings, of the two suitors, and of the subject-matter in dispute, of the assembly of Kentish men to form the shire court of Kent.

Now about these two records of meetings of the shire—one in the reign of Canute, the other in that of William the Conqueror; one relating to Hereford-shire, the other to Kent—there is one thing quite clear: they are, in all essentials and allowing for the increased power of the Norman sovereign, identical in the facts they reveal of the ancient shire-moot. It was a court of shiremen for shiremen; it was a primary assembly—that is, an assembly composed of the entire community entitled to attend, instead of an assembly composed of elected representatives; it took cognizance of pleadings for land which had not, therefore, been transferred to the king's courts; it met as all ancient tribal courts met, and as they meet now where the tribal system has survived, and it was independent. The very beginnings of a new system, when local justice was to become king's justice, is plainly seen in the later record—beginnings which were not carried further towards completed fact until Henry II., at the Council of Northampton, divided the kingdom into six circuits, appointed a judge for each circuit, and attached the shires to them.

I do not want for the purpose of these lectures to trace out the changes in the government of the shire from the Conquest to 1888; still it is necessary to state a few of the salient points. Bishop Stubbs has succinctly described its functions in the reign of Edward I. (*Const. Hist.*, ii. 208-216), and it is clear that the whole business of the shire—judicial, police, military, remedial measures, fiscal and political—were conducted in the court of the shire, presided over by the shire-reeve, or sheriff, and constituted by the men of the shire, suitors to the court. The shire has by this time become the county. Even from the purely legal aspect, always, as it seems to me, somewhat short of the historical aspect, the county was not a mere stretch of land, a governmental district—it was an organized body of men, a communitas; and if legally we must stop short of saying it was a corporation, "the law and the language of the period seem at first sight to treat counties very much as though they were corporations." Under Edward I. the county of Devon had a common seal, and John granted to Cornwall and Devonshire charters which in point of form differed little from those he granted to boroughs. I shall sum up the legal position of the county in the words of Sir Frederick Pollock and Mr. Maitland: "The actual assembly of men sitting at a certain time and place to hear causes is the county; the permanent institution of which that particular assembly is, as it were, a fleeting representation is the county; the county, again, is a tract of ground; the county is the whole body of persons who hold lands or reside within that tract, whether they participate in the doings of the representative assembly or not" (*Hist. of English Law*, i. 521). This composite character of the county, at once a territory and a community of persons, an assembly or council and a communitas in the general sense, is of great importance. It marks the unassimilated elements which come partly from primitive and partly from later institutions, that is to say the tribal element, based upon personal relationship, and the political element, based upon territorial relationship.

Nothing in this legal description of the county of Edward the First's reign separates it from the shire of Edward the Confessor's reign, and the changes which follow are changes in the constitution of its assembly, or court, not changes in the territorium, not in the locality which we understand in reference to local government. The changes are due to several causes. First, the king's courts at Westminster took cognizance of legal cases, and questions of title to land were the first to be transferred. In personal actions the limit of forty shillings appears general in the reign of Edward I., and the economical value of this limit, gradually lessening each century, has correspondingly lessened the jurisdiction of the court. The attendance of shiremen at the court was looked upon as a heavy burden, not as a privilege, and the successive Acts of Parliament which have placed the business of the county in the hands of commissioners appointed by the Crown were in thorough accord with the trend of the times. Thus the Pipe Roll of Henry I. proves the existence of large bodies of judices and juratores at the county courts, but the sheriffs' accounts contain some significant entries. Those of Yorkshire state that the judges and jurors of Yorkshire owe a hundred pounds that they may no more be judges or jurors. Now when we remember that the ancient principle was to fine members for non-attendance, it is plain that here the fine was losing its significance and object as a payment to *compel* attendance, and was becoming a payment frankly accepted in lieu of attendance.

The institution of circuits for fiscal purposes by Henry I., the extension of judicial duties to these circuits by Henry II., mark this decline of the shiremoot. Then we come to the office of coroner, which was instituted in 1194. He was to be elected by the landholders of the county, not by the shire court, a fact which, far from pointing to a fresh expression of popular rights, as is generally supposed, seems to me to mark the introduction of new forces. The shire court, like all early assemblies, had, hitherto, had the control and election of its own officers, but it had ceased to meet as an assembly of the shire. It did not meet as all the men of the shire; it was never made a representative body, and so the men of the shire elected their coroner without formally meeting at a shire assembly. And thus the way was prepared for fresh innovation. The responsibility for peace had rested with the old shire-moot, but in the 1st of Edward III. an enactment was made that good and lawful men should be commissioned to keep the peace in each county. Gradually one new duty after another was imposed upon the justices of the peace, as they were soon called, until, in the end, they have been looked upon as the sole county authority. At one critical stage it seemed as if they might have become the direct and only taxing authority. They were intrusted with the direct taxation of county inhabitants, instead of assessing the parishes, in 1530 and in 1531; the first for the repair of bridges, the second for the erection of jails. But this was the last experiment in this innovating system—a system which would have destroyed local government in the county, for it would have separated the right of taxation from the right of representation. Although county justices sent their precepts down to the parishes for the taxation necessary to meet county expenditure, the amount has always been small, and the indirect method of getting at the taxpayer has kept attention from the subject.

Still, with all the changes, the ancient territorium of the county and the assembly, or court, of the county has never ceased to have continuous life. This is shown in a most picturesque detail thus described in the language of lawyers as it obtained in the reign of Edward I.: "One act of jurisdiction, one supreme and solemn act, could be performed only in the county court, and in the folk-moot of London—the act of outlawry" (Pollock and Maitland, *Hist. of English Law*, i. 540). Now this act of outlawry goes back to the most primitive period of Teutonic history, to the laws of tribesmen before they had become identified with special territories, those tribesmen of whom I have already spoken as originating the shires, and it comes down to modern times, when John Wilkes was outlawed in the county court of Middlesex, "at the Three Tons, in Brook Street, near Holborne, in the county of Middlesex" (Burrow's Reports, p. 2530).

Let me note another factor in the history of the county which seems to me to suggest the continuous existence of its ancient form of assembly. Until recent times "the knights of the shire" elected to the House of Commons were freeholders elected from the freeholders in open hustings. These freeholders are the constitutional descendants of the thanes who formed the shire assembly in Canute's time and in William's time; and, though I cannot discover any special points illustrating the connection of the hustings with the county, it is not altogether devoid of significance to point out that in this word husting—house-thing—we have an ancient Scandinavian form of the name of the assembly. What, then, was the hustings? It was the assembly of the county for the purpose of electing one of its members to the parliament of the nation. The place of assembly was often the ancient place of assembly of the shire-moot, and it will appeal to your sense of continuity in these things when I point out that the hustings of the county of Kent were held on Pennenden Heath, near Maidstone, exactly on the spot where the shire assembly of 1072 was held, and where the County Hall of to-day stands; and I like to recall the fact that I spent one memorable day in the library of the late Professor Stanley Jevons in finding out that the hustings of the county of Middlesex were held on Hampstead Heath, near the spot which contains the ancient so-called barrow and Parliament Hill.

One other detail gives evidence of the continuous life of the shire as a local government area—namely, its existence as a taxing unit. Under the Anglo-Saxon system each shire was bound to furnish ships in proportion to its number of hundreds, and from the produce of what had been the folkland contained in it it had to pay a composition for the sustentation of the king (Stubbs, *Const. Hist.*, i. 116). Much of this is lost sight of after the Conquest, but, as Mr. Thorold Rogers very acutely remarks, "the convention of taxpayers" must have been held before the great charters of John and Henry, and the only machinery then available was the shire organization. Stripped of much of its local administrative powers, it was still powerful as a taxing unit, and even amidst all the changes that have taken place it is still the ancient taxing unit for one of the imperial taxes, namely, the land tax.

It is worth while summing up this evidence of continuity in the shire and its ancient assembly. Premising that this ancient assembly was not elected, but consisted of all the thanes, or freeholders of the shire, we have noted (1) that the freeholders up to 1888 elected the coroner of the county; (2) that the freeholders elected the knight of the shire to serve in Parliament, and formally met at the hustings to perform this act; (3) that the right of outlawry, one of the ancient tribal rights of the shire, remains with the shire to the present day, and was last exercised in the case of John Wilkes, in 1764; (4) that the county, one of the ancient taxing units, has remained a taxing unit until to-day. If I were to affirm that the right of the shire, or county, to assemble for constitutional purposes had never been taken away by statute or other formal act of sovereignty; if I pointed to the corresponding right of assembly in the borough and in the township or parish (about which I shall have to speak later on); and if I went on to say that this right of assembly still existed, and could still be invoked, I should, no doubt, be met by legal arguments as to the non-effective force of custom which had been so long dormant, and possibly by some legal decisions, or by some statutory provisions; but, though the astuteness of lawyers may effectually put a full stop at any stage in the legal history of these matters, I do not admit that they can stay the constitutional history.

The long period of gradual decline of county government corresponds to a period of stagnation in local government generally. We get glimpses of attempts to use the commissions of county magistrates for various purposes, and the administration of the poor law was first placed in their hands. But no serious attempt to use the splendid organization of the county in the government of the country was possible until it was taken out of the hands of commissioners appointed by the Crown and again placed in the hands of the shiremen. This, and nothing short of it, is what was accomplished by the Act of 1888. There was, under that Act, no *creation* of county councils, still less was there a *creation* of county government. There has only been a restoration to the locality of the county of a representative form of government, in place of the open gathering of all shiremen which it formerly possessed. Nothing is more important than to remember this. All the administrative powers of the justices were transferred to the county council, and the justices inherited these powers from the ancient county courts. There was no actual break. The time had come for this change. New functions of government were being created, which needed some form of local authority to carry them out; and the form selected by the Parliament of 1888 was the ancient form of county government. That the Act extended this ancient form of government and this ancient territorial formation to special areas, like the three ridings of Yorkshire, the ancient divisions of Holland, Kesteven and Lindsey, in Lincolnshire, the soke of Peterborough, the Isle of Wight, East and West Suffolk, East and West Sussex, and, finally, to the remarkable community which is gathered round the City of London, is only the application of ancient principles of local government to modern developments—it is not in reality a fresh creation. The pity of it is that this wise and politic reform should not have been thoroughly carried out; should have been clogged with such a meaningless adjective as "administrative," and should have left many of the old county elements still alive, to the confusion of our school manuals and the everlasting trouble of people who cannot approach a new idea untrammelled by what they themselves have been used to—those people, I mean, who still talk of London as the metropolis, who would still deny her the unity and dignity of her county organization and rank. Even Government departments—nay, even the

Local Government Board—are not yet fully aware that London is a county. Because a little tongue of land at the southern boundary—the hamlet of Penge—is in the Croydon Union for poor-law purposes—that is to say, because the county of London, like every other county in the kingdom, without a single exception, is cut into by different poor-law unions, instead of containing a certain number of poor-law unions—it is constantly stated, and in official documents, that the hamlet of Penge is not in the county of London. The statement is ridiculous. Penge, like every other hamlet, township, or parish, in the area defined by the Act of 1888, is a part of the county of London, and it only differs from other parishes or hamlets in the county in that the poor-law system, not being founded according to the principles of local government, includes it in a union which cuts across the county boundary.

This leads me to say one word about another sort of county which has found its way into statistics—that is, into the census and into the Local Government Board returns: the so-called registration county. This absolutely meaningless unit has been foisted into local government simply because it is a convenient term to apply to certain aggregations of poor-law areas. All the poor-law areas which for the most part are contained in any given county are called the "registration county" of the same name as the true county, although in no single instance is it conterminous with the true county. Thus the so-called registration county of London excludes the London parish of Penge; the so-called registration county of Surrey includes the London parish of Penge, the Hampshire parishes of Aldershot and Dockenfield, and the Middlesex parishes of Hampton, Hampton Wick, and Teddington, while, on the other hand, it excludes its own Surrey parishes of Lingfield, which is taken over by Sussex, and Thorpe and Egham, which are taken over by Berkshire. Thus we have to talk of a London which is not London, and a Surrey which is not Surrey. And so it is all over the kingdom, there is not a single so-called registration county which is a true county. And the reason for all this confusion is that the registration of births, deaths, and marriages is performed through the machinery of the poor-law system,—with which, however, it has absolutely nothing whatever to do,—and must, therefore, be grouped according to the poor-law system. It would be interesting to know how many thousands of pounds this grouping has cost the nation at the time of each census, and how much money is wasted in producing results which are absolutely confusing. It would be still more interesting to enquire when Parliament will awake to these strange and absurd anomalies, which deny to counties their proper organization for registration and all purposes simply because a system has grown up of making the poor-law system the basis of registration.

I have now, I hope sufficiently, dealt with local government in the counties, and particularly with the important point of continuity—an absolute continuity so far as locality is concerned, a relative continuity so far as government is concerned ; and I point out here how great has been the influence of *locality* in preserving the forms of county government. We have the locality first, the communitas of the locality next, the elected governing authority of the locality last. It is the fashion of to-day to speak overmuch of the governing authority, and not at all of the locality and the communitas of the locality. Statesmen allow themselves to speak of county councils as if they were a body apart from the ratepayers of the county. The old forms should be remembered and restored. Officers of county councils are county officers. We still have " Clerk of the Peace for the County," " County Surveyor," " County Treasurer." We should keep to this formula, and have " County Clerk " to parallel with " Town Clerk," " County Engineer," " County Valuer," " County Comptroller," and so on ; because officers are servants of the county—not of that small portion of the county which is elected to perform its administrative business.

This part of the subject makes clear the status of

the county and its government. We have next to consider its relationship to other local authorities—its *rank*, in point of fact.

The records are not clear and consistent enough for us to be certain that the shire court was a court of appeal from the township court, but so long as the " four men and the reeve" from each township were the representatives of the townships in the shire court, it seems hardly possible to argue that whatever business could not be attended to in the lesser courts, and all business which involved the interests of two or more townships, was not *ipso facto* conducted in the shire court.

Mr. Kemble's terminology is now no longer accepted by scholars as true to the English evidence, but there is no reason to doubt his conclusions when they relate to general constitutional matters. He puts it that the shire " was able to do right between Mark and Mark [*i.e.*, township and township] as well as between man and man, and to decide those differences the arrangement of which transcended the powers of the smaller body " (*Saxons in England*, i. 73).

I am sure you have not missed the significance of all this ancient constitutional life of the shire or county in connection with our modern county government. The county comes to us from the centuries gone by, as an independent unit of an amalgamated territory, and not as the division by monarch or Parliament of a territory for the purpose of administrative machinery, to be allotted just what powers and functions it pleased the State government to allot and change from time to time. There is all the difference in the world between these two origins. The independent origin would carry with it rights, customs, duties, and privileges which the legislative origin would not, and the elasticity of the former condition would allow of the accretion of further rights, customs, duties, and privileges as time and events marched on. And let it be noted that, although the ancient shire system of government was very early under the Norman rule superseded by the system of commission, the shire itself as a distinct locality, with distinct rights of taxation, has never been superseded.

I should like next to interpose a word or two about the hundred, which has dropped out of local institutions. Like the county, it was an ancient tribal formation; but, unlike the county, it was formed for purposes of police and of military organization by the aggregation of the smaller township units. Like the county, its historical names were not derived from the towns, but were independent names applied to the hundred area. Like the county, it had an assembly which was judicial as well as legislative; and, like the county, it was one of the most ancient taxing areas. But its fortune has been different to that of the county. It has never been used for the purposes of modern civilization, and it has been allotted as private franchises to feudal lords—as, for instance, the forest court of Knaresborough.

There is one ancient attribute of the hundred, however, which was only abolished in 1888 and transferred to the counties. This was its collective liability for damage to property within its area, by riot or other form of impersonal action. Thus when Nottingham Castle was burnt by the mob in 1832 the hundred was sued, and the owners recovered damages to the amount of £21,000. Within two or three years prior to 1888 destruction of property at elections has come upon the hundred, and ratepayers, as Professor Earle says, have had occasion to learn that the hundred was not dead (Earle's *Land Charters*, p. 50). This collective liability is very instructive. Historically it takes us back to the hundred as a community of persons, rather than a territory of ratepayers. Politically it gives us a form of "collectivism" which is singularly free from criticism by those who would banish all forms of collectivism to the planets; but probably collective liability is one thing, and collective operations to benefit the community a totally different thing. In any case the form of collectivism presented by the liability of the hundred now resides in the county, and I will read to you the clause of the Act of 1888 (79 (2)) which makes this so: "All duties and liabilities of the inhabitants of a county shall become and be duties and liabilities of the council of such county." I think the obvious importance and significance of this clause are not thoroughly understood by our modern "men of the county," and later on I shall have to refer to this collective liability of the county in connection with a power which ought to reside in the county.

III

LOCALITIES (*continued*)—BOROUGHS

MY next subject is the Borough, and here, I think, I shall give you a little more trouble than with the county.

In questions of origin there is, of course, no distinction between county boroughs and ordinary municipal boroughs. That distinction is due entirely to the Act of 1888, and simply means boroughs which have the full organization of a county, and are not, therefore, represented on the county councils, and boroughs which possess something less than the full organization of a county, and are, therefore, represented on the county councils.

The Act of 1888 produced, indeed, a very sensible effect upon municipal organization, and I propose before touching upon the question of origin to classify the boroughs as they now stand in relation to the legal status created by the Act of 1888. There are three classes of boroughs—county boroughs, boroughs having a population of over 10,000, and boroughs having a population of under 10,000. The county boroughs even are not all equal, because eighteen do not possess exclusive jurisdiction, the following not possessing separate quarter sessions:—Barrow, Bootle, Burnley, Bury, Cardiff, Coventry, Gateshead, Halifax, Huddersfield, Middlesborough, Rochdale, St. Helens, South Shields, Stockport, Sunderland, Swansea, West Bromwich, and West Ham; and one—Barrow—does not possess a separate commission of the peace. Again, Croydon, West Ham, Bury, Dudley, Gloucester and West Bromwich do not possess their own borough police force.

Of the second class of boroughs, some have lost their ancient power to appoint separate coroners and maintain separate police forces; while of the third class, twenty-eight still retain their quarter sessions.

On the other hand, there are three cities which are not incorporated as boroughs,—Llandaff, Ely, and St. David's—and six county towns—Aylesbury, Oakham, Dolgelly, Welshpool, Newtown, and Presteign. The number of districts having a population of over 10,000, and, therefore, the initial qualification for the dignity of borough, is no less than 166; but the Local Government Act of 1894, which raised them, except those situated in the county of London, to the status of district council, will probably prevent charters of incorporation being granted to these towns, except in very important cases.

This difference in status is a modern growth. It denotes nothing as to origin. In order to discuss this,

I will first recall to your attention the description of the burgh of the Anglo-Saxon period given by Bishop Stubbs. It was, he says, "simply a more strictly organized form of the township; it was probably in a more defensible position, had a ditch and mound, instead of the quickset hedge, or 'tun,' from which the township took its name; and, as the 'tun' originally was the fenced homestead of the cultivator, the burh was the fortified house and courtyard of the mighty man—the king, the magistrate, or the noble. . . . Other towns grew up round the country-houses of the kings and ealdormen, round the great monasteries in which the bishops had their seats, and in such situations as were pointed out by nature as suited for trade and commerce."

Bishop Stubbs, in writing this lucid description of the origin of the burgh, expressly precludes any connection between the burghs of the Anglo-Saxons and remains of Roman civilization. But I shall have to point out, even for the limited purpose of these lectures, that such preclusion is not warranted by the evidence. I have elsewhere dealt somewhat minutely with the evidence of Roman origins in connection with the early municipal history of London (*The Village Community*, pp. 208, *et seq*), and I cannot do more than direct your attention to this in proof of my proposition that some of the Roman cities, at all events, were the originals of the burghs that grew up under Anglo-

Saxon civilization. I do not want to make more of this than is necessary, and I do not suggest that occupation of the Roman site necessarily meant continuity of occupation from Roman times, still less continuity of Roman institutions. But, all the same, the burghs founded on Roman sites are as a rule different in important characteristics from those growing up on English sites.

I, therefore, class the burghs into two divisions— those originating in the more successful and better defended townships, and those originating in Roman sites. Now the first question arising in a consideration of what the English burgh was has reference to the territorium of the burgh; and here we are met, not only with the historical distinction just noted, but with legal difficulties. I must first state these legal difficulties. The earliest charters are grants of privileges and franchises to the burgesses and citizens of the particular borough, and not until the reign of Richard II. are we confronted with the legal problem presented by the holding of lands. Then the Government seem to have learnt for the first time that the burghs were like the religious bodies, against whom the Statutes of Mortmain had been passed, capable of holding lands; for the famous statute of 15th Richard II. (1391) seems to me not only to have taken a singularly long time in finding its place upon the Statute Book, but its wording implies the idea of a recent discovery. This Act begins by reciting the former prohibitions against religious houses holding lands in perpetuity, extends that prohibition to guilds and fraternities, and afterwards adds that "because mayors, bailiffs, and commons of cities, boroughs, and other towns which have a perpetual commonalty, and others which have offices perpetual, be as perpetual as people of religion, they shall not thenceforth purchase to them and to their commons and offices." Here the significance surely lies in the frank recognition of the corporate character of perpetual succession and in the prohibition "thenceforth," implying that up to that time boroughs possessed or had attained lands, but were not to do so in the future without legal sanction—in other words, unless they were incorporated.

A great deal has been made of this question of incorporation, but I do not think it is altogether a matter of law. We want to know how the law arose, and under what circumstances it was first applied. Knowing the date when the English municipalities were first incorporated, what we have to ascertain is what were the circumstances which led to this change of constitution. Now whatever were the influences which produced municipal boroughs on English soil, those influences were English, and the municipal system was English;

and whatever were the influences which brought about legal incorporation, those influences were Norman; but the conception of incorporation came from the Roman law. Here, then, are two opposite influences at work, and here lies the key to the problem. The Roman municipium was a *corpus*, or corporation, and held its territorium in right of its legal position; it was called into existence by the sovereign government — that is, by a *senatûs-consultum*, by a *lex*, or by an Imperial constitution. The question, then, is, how were these two opposite systems of polity—the English and the Roman—brought together? Fifteenth-century lawyers awake to the facts of Roman law, fifteenth-century monarchs, anxious to extend their sovereignty, combined to bring the English burghs within the four corners of this legal conception; and they began the process, not by wholesale grants of incorporation to burghs which were not incorporated, but by a disabling Act, to bring sharp home to them what incorporation might mean. Burghs were made to understand that they could not acquire property unless they were incorporated.

I think this course is most significant. A formal grant of incorporation would not have been thought much of by burghs which had existed without it for centuries. London, for instance, which in Athelstan's reign possessed a code —*judicia civi-*

tatis Lundoniæ, which provided that half the property of a convicted thief was to go to the king, and half to the reeveshire—that is, to the ward over which the reeve presided—had already provided for municipal property; Canterbury, with its "*urbana prata*," its "*burgwara mædum*" (*Codex Dip.*, ii. 26, 66) of pre-Domesday times, and its burgess houses held at the time of Domesday "*in gildam suam*"— *i.e.*, in their corporate capacity (Coote, *Romans of Britain*, 376); other burghs similarly placed, and there were many, would not understand the needs of incorporation based on an appeal to philosophical jurisprudence. Their understanding, therefore, was sharpened by the Act of Richard II., and incorporation became to them a legal necessity.

Still the process was slow. Legal incorporation was not granted as a privilege until 1439, when Kingston-upon-Hull and Plymouth were incorporated—the first by charter, the second by statute. Henry VI. also gave grants of incorporation to Ipswich, Southampton, Coventry, Northampton, Woodstock, Canterbury, Nottingham, and Tenterden. These grants, however, did not become general, for Norwich, Bristol, and the Cinque Ports received charters without incorporation from Edward IV., who, on the other hand, conferred this privilege on Rochester, Stamford, Ludlow, Grantham, Wenlock, Bewdley, and Kingston. The question of incorporation is further complicated by the contention of the boroughs about this period that, though not expressly incorporated, this right must be presumed from the circumstances of their creation, and must, therefore, have been conferred by some grant beyond legal memory; and in the year 1466 it was actually held by the Court of Common Pleas that words of incorporation might be implied in a grant " if the king gave land in fee-farm to the good men of the town, . . . and so likewise where it was given to the burgesses, citizens, and commonalty " (Merewether and Stephens, 37–8). Thus, important as incorporation is from the legal point of view, we have the following condition of things to show that the law lagged behind the facts: (1) that in Richard II.'s reign English lawyers discovered that boroughs were practically corporations, from which position they were dislodged by special Act of Parliament; (2) that Edward IV. granted incorporation in a fashion so erratic as to show, at least, a want of appreciation of its importance by the boroughs; (3) that the boroughs claimed to be incorporated without a charter to that express effect.

I want now to place before you a statement of the position of the burghs from the historical point of view, and I want then to summarize the evidence which exists, and to apply it to the problem presented by this double standpoint of history and law.

LOCAL GOVERNMENT

The first thing to note is that the economic conditions of the Roman cities and of the Anglo-Saxon tribes who conquered these cities were on a different plane—the former was the advanced economical system of an empire, such as the British Empire of to-day ; the latter was the primitive economical system of tribal society, such as the Hindu tribes of to-day. At no point did they touch or converge ; at no point could the one naturally or instinctively carry on the work of the other. At all points they were antagonistic.

Between the life in the Roman cities and the life in the English burghs there is a gap, therefore, which cannot be bridged over by the simple theory of historic continuity. Nevertheless, the gap is lessened by the influence which the Roman cities had upon the development of English burghal life. The destruction of the Roman cities did not mean the destruction of the conditions which had made the Roman cities what they were, whenever the time was ripe for such conditions to again arise. The quickened development of Anglo-Saxon life on British soil brought these conditions into being towards the end of the Anglo-Saxon period ; and as a result the sites of old Roman cities became here and there the sites of English burghs, occasionally, as in London for certain, carrying on the old Roman mercantile law and principles, and, as at York, Gloucester,

Chester, Bath, Dorchester, Colchester, and elsewhere, carrying on some of the traditions of Roman life. But not everywhere did these conditions apply. At Silchester, for instance, the Calleva Atrebatum of the Romans, we have a signal example of a destroyed Roman city never again restored to life. You can walk round its walls, go through its gates, stand on the tesselated pavements of its forum, its temple and its houses; walk down its streets and across the very ruts made in the roadway by Roman carts; and you may still see the amphitheatre outside its walls, still trace the great roadways converging to it as to a centre. But the Saxon plough has been driven over it, and on the site where Roman municipal life went on English corn is now growing. Then there are such significant cases as St. Albans, which was not built upon the Roman site, still desolate and undeveloped, and still known as Verulam, but was built just alongside and out of the ruins of the Roman city.

On the other hand, English burghs grew up on native English sites—that is, sites developed entirely by the economical conditions of English life. This amounts to saying that the Teutons, like the Romans, the Greeks, and other branches of the same race to which Teutons, Romans, and Greeks alike belong, developed in due course the city form of political organization, as well as the State form. This parallel takes us further on than is sometimes supposed. Thus there are the signs of political independence which the burghs of England gave promise of at the time of the Norman Conquest and later—London, in claiming and obtaining an independent voice in the formal election of the king, and in the long-continued theory of independence which is illustrated by the well-known custom of closing the city gates at the death of every king, and only proclaiming the new monarch within her walls after admission has been formally asked and obtained; Exeter, in raising the standard of independent existence when William had already conquered the country; the five Danish burghs, Lincoln, Nottingham, Derby, Leicester, and Stamford, which had not only special privileges of their own, but a common organization apparently of the nature of a confederation; and the Cinque Ports, whose confederation was a matter of almost recent history. And there are the peculiar combinations of the Scottish burghs, which existed from the days of David I.—one consisting of Aberdeen and the burghs northwards, under a confederacy called by the name of Hanse; the other a sort of burghal parliament, called *Curia Quatuor Burgorum*, composed of delegates of the burghs of Berwick, Roxburgh, Edinburgh, and Sterling.

Mr. Freeman has suggested that such early combinations, or confederacies, of burghs bring the course of development in English constitutional life to a converging point with Greek constitutional life, from which other influences only just succeeded in preventing a parallel development, when the city organization would have been the foundation of the English constitution, and not the State organization. I think the suggestion opens up a fruitful source of special enquiry not yet undertaken by any student of English municipal history, and I think it accounts for some of the conditions of English towns up to the end of the Middle Ages. For my present purpose I ask you to remember that the State organization under which we live is not the only form of national existence ; and that the city organization, which made Greek life what it was, which was the foundation of Roman life, has had a history, though a brief one, in English life.

The question is, Does this development of English city life amount to more than this—more, I mean, not in the sense of the comparative importance between English and other forms of city life in European peoples, but in the sense of developing a peculiarly English form of city life? I think the adaptation of the burghs and the counties to the military organization, which is more or less popularly connected with the name of the great Saxon king Alfred, is the answer which meets us from the mists of history, though not sufficiently clearly to be able to formulate the precise factors which may thus be reckoned as specially English.[1] Still this point must not be lost sight of, and accordingly when summarizing the elements which make up the burghal organization to be examined by the historian they will be found to consist of—(1) common Aryan influences, (2) Romano-British influences, and (3) English influences.

I hope I have stated the legal position and the historical position with sufficient clearness, even if I have not been able to state them in greater detail. My next task is to apply to these two positions the details of English burghal life as it has come down to us.

These details are—(1) ceremonial, (2) constitutional, (3) economical, (4) social.

I dismiss the first, or ceremonial, division, tempting though it is to dwell upon, with the observation that municipal ceremonial contains many features of extremely archaic character parallel in a remarkable degree to archaic ceremonial belonging to English institutions other than municipal, and to institutions which are neither municipal nor English, in Germany, Russia, and other homes of ancient Aryan life.

The social division scarcely concerns us at all.

---

[1] Since this lecture was delivered Professor Maitland has worked this point up with most remarkable success in his work on Domesday Book, and I have summarized my own views thereon on p. 46 *ante*.

And this leaves for consideration the constitutional and economical divisions. In respect of these I omit all matters which do not bear upon the immediate purpose of these lectures. At some time or other, by some means or other, which have escaped the ken of history, but which we cannot doubt have followed the almost inevitable law of analogy—like causes producing like results—the condition of burgess-ship was created in Anglo-Saxon times. The question is, what was its fundamental basis? There is evidence that the ancient tribal basis of kinship by blood obtained in the rural communities of Britain in early times, and even lasted down to late times, a manorial tenant of King's Repton in 1296, for instance, being stated to be of the blood of the manor—*de sanguine de Repton Regis*; and I have discussed this point in my book on the Village Community. But the cement which bound burgesses together was distinctly not that of kinship by blood.

In 1890 I pointed out—I believe for the first time—the curious importance of certain entries in Domesday. To many of the manors are said to belong certain burgesses. Thus, among the Wiltshire boroughs, in Wilton there were five burgesses of Nigrave, seven of Sarisberie, one of Stradford, two of Fifhide, one of Come, four of Diarneford, one of Scarentone, one of Meresdene, and one of Odestoke; in Cricklade there were six burgesses of

Aldeborne, five of Ramesberie, one of Badeberie, one of Piritone, six of Chiseldene, one of Ledentone, seven of Lediar, three of Clive, and three of Colecote, and so on. In seeking for the origin of this curious relationship between burgh and manor, one must look to economical causes, not legal or constitutional, and an important parallel is presented in modern Russia, where members of the mir frequently go to the towns to work, while retaining, and ultimately returning to claim, all the privileges of their ancestral rights in their native village. Though these Russian townsmen work in the towns, they really belong to the mir; economically they have been thrust forward to meet the necessities of burghal development, constitutionally they have been kept back to meet the traditional reverence for tribal ties. The continental picture drawn by Bishop Agobardus of men standing side by side in cities and large towns, each one of whom is governed by a different law, law being incidental, not to the locality, but to the person, flowing, not from the sovereign of the country, but from the kinship which binds together the descendants of a common ancestor, may have been reproduced in England when the villans of manors, believing that they belonged to the blood of the manor, went to work in the burghs, especially as there are traces of it in the constitution of the Gilds, as Mr. Ashley has pointed out (*Economic History*, i. 75).

In any case the Domesday burgesses were not kinsmen to each other; and if an appeal is made to comparative politics, Mr. Freeman's main conclusions are all that remain as a guide to determine the cement which bound burgess to burgess. The civic franchise, whatever it might have been worth, and whatever it carried with it, could be had only by the appointed means. It did not belong to every man who chose to go and dwell within the civic boundary. It might not always be purely a matter of birth, but it was always something which could not be taken up at the mere will of the stranger. It was always acquired by that particular qualification which was fixed by the custom of the civic community, be that qualification birth, marriage, servitude, special purchase or special grant (Freeman's *Comparative Politics*, 283). Here, then, are the elements of contract, not status, of a political combination, not a tribal, of an economical basis, not a kinship basis; and it is from this starting-point, lost though it is in English evidence, that the origin of English burghal life must be considered.

Just let me for one moment illustrate the growth of the idea of a burghal community as distinct from an indeterminate mass of burgesses. In 762 a house (villa) was sold at Canterbury, "*cum tributo illius possidendum*" (*Cod. Dip.*, i. 133). In 857 a house (*haga*) was sold in London for twelve pence (*Cod.*

Dip., ii. 63). These two transactions indicate individual action among the burgesses. If this is the earliest glimpse we can get of the action of burgesses, a great change is marked towards the end of the Saxon period. Before the Norman Conquest it appears from Domesday that the *firma burgi*—that is, a permanently fixed sum—was paid by the body of burgesses in lieu of individual assessments. I am aware that lawyers, as a rule, deny that the *firma burgi* is any evidence of a corporate act, but so good a lawyer as my friend the late Henry Charles Coote maintained it was a sure sign of a corporate act, and the same contention was passionately advocated by the late Mr. Toulmin Smith. At all events, I think the transition from individual to collective payment indicates a change in the fiscal relationship of the burgesses to each other which could only have been brought about by an already existing basis, whatever that basis might have been, of communal interests.

I next turn to the economical evidence. Nearly eighteen years ago I discussed this subject, writing then under the influence of Sir Henry Maine's works. Coming back again to it now, one factor of supreme importance which was clearly shown by the evidence collected by the Municipal Commissioners of 1835 was that the English boroughs were land-owning communities. Faulty as this evidence unfortunately is in detail, it supplies what could not be supplied by any other method—the exact conditions of land tenure at a given date. If these conditions had been uniform—if all municipalities had possessed lands and let them out at rack-rents, according to the modern principles of economics—there would not have been much to say about the significance of municipal land-ownership. But this was not the case. Some let their lands out at rack-rents; some possessed rights of pasturage only, and burgesses used these rights; some possessed meadow land, which was allotted year by year among the burgesses, and after harvest thrown into common; some possessed, together with pasturage, arable lands, which were allotted year by year among the burgesses, and after harvest thrown into common; one or two possessed large tracts of land, which were cultivated by the burgesses in a fashion which can only be described by the term extremely archaic. I am sure you do not miss the significance of evidence such as this, and will not be surprised at the argument I used eighteen years ago—that this overlapping of different classes of municipal land tenure pointed to unequal developments from an original system which at one time prevailed amongst all the municipalities alike, and that this system was that of the village community.

Now how far does this help us to understand the burghal organization? The answer is to be found in the ancient principle that the right to allotments in the common fields surrounding the homestead depended upon the holding of a tenement in the village. Instances are found in early times. Thus in 832 King Æthelwulf grants a *haga* (house) in Canterbury, to which are attached, "*ad quam pertinet*" (*sic*), five acres of arable, two meadows and common wood (*Cod. Dip.*, v. 88), and I interpret in the same manner the references to property in Winchester (*Cod. Dip.*, vi. 33), and in London (*Cod. Dip.*, iv. 211), to which was attached land in the shire. This selfsame right has very extensively survived in municipal custom. In the remarkable instance of the Burgh of Lauder, no one can be a burgess who does not possess a "burgess acre," and the possession of these acres carries with it a right to "the outfield and freeland parts thereto belonging as the same shall happen to fall by cut and cavil." According to the ancient custumal of Preston, "no one can be a burgess unless he have a burgage of twelve feet in front," and this burgage carries with it land rights. The first charter to Salford distinctly recognises the same right. As a matter of fact, these modern survivals are met with in almost all our chief borough towns—not, it is true, in the exact form of the archaic model given in these instances, but in the more general form of the burgesses occupying ancient burgage tenements. A large part of the city of Gloucester is corporation property, and this holding of burgage property is extant in very many towns, among which I may mention Marlborough, Newbury, Tewkesbury, Worcester, Alnwick, nearly all the Welsh boroughs, and many more which it will not perhaps be necessary to enumerate.

The importance of the burgage tenement is again shown by the ancient custom at Folkestone, Hastings, and London of an offence against the community being punished by the house of the offender being publicly demolished by the commonalty, while at Preston a debtor to the king's ferm was liable to have the door of his burgage tenement taken away, which he could not replace until his debt was paid. Here the burgage tenement is clearly a symbol of the burgage right.

Now I come to the last point, and it is this—namely, that the owners of burgage tenements were the burgesses, and that the whole body of burgesses—not a selected few, not an elected body—composed the municipality, were, indeed, the burghal assembly. The duties of this assembly are sufficiently significant in the burghs which still held their lands for agricultural purposes before the general Reform Act. Thus the burgh assemblies at Lauder, Berwick-on-Tweed, Malmesbury, Beccles, Laughearne, and other places made by-laws, regulated the enjoyment of the meadows and stints, prescribed the conditions of husbandry, and decided the right of claimants to a share in the allotments.

This evidence, if I mistake not, suggests a new and important view for considering the origin of English burghs. A very distinguished legal scholar, Professor Maitland, has challenged my views as to the archaic origin of the burghal constitution by advancing some legal difficulties which I have been bound to examine, and I confess that my mode of treating this part of my subject has been dictated, to some extent, by the criticism given to it by Professor Maitland. I am confronted with the charters which do not grant land, with the "mass of men who are the burgesses for the time being," enjoying lands in co-ownership as distinguished from ownership by a community, with the legal difficulty of conceiving anything but a legal condition of things. But the mass of men who were burgesses was not a legal creation, and yet they massed, and organized, and developed, not towards an individual type, but towards a communal type, and, finally, compelled English law to take note of them and to endow them with corporate life. The evidence begins in the early history of economics, not in that of law; it continues its course through the early history of the State organization, during which time the chances of a city organization were very great; it finishes in the history of Norman sovereignty and the growth of Norman law. This evidence shows us the village community as the groundwork of all. The development of burghal life from this groundwork took two courses—one where the village community absorbed much of the free tribal institutions, and simply developed into the burghs, of which Lauder, in Berwickshire, and Malmesbury, in Wilts, are the types; the second where the village community became subordinate, not to the free tribe, as it did generally throughout Teutonic Britain, not to the lord, as it did in later times, and of which the manor is the well-known type, but to the new industrial or commercial community—the burghers, in fact. Here we have the dual element of agricultural serfdom under a higher organization which is free, which is the distinguishing feature of the village community system, only it introduces a type not hitherto noted by scholars—namely, the burghal type, which consists of the free burghers at the top of the organism, with the village community at the bottom of the organism.

I am afraid you will think I have somewhat gone off the main line at this juncture, but that is not the case. The boroughs of England are so important a feature of local government that it is all-important to understand their true place. If their prominent position in mediæval times brought them under the cognizance of the law, it did not reduce all their rights and customs to the position of positive law, and it is from these rights and customs that I have drawn the conclusions as to the burgess organization being formed by an adaptation of the ancient system of the tribe and the village community to the new developments of commerce. The bearing of this upon the particular points of interest to us has relation to the principle of *locality* in local government, and I will proceed to show how this is.

The boundaries of all the prescriptive boroughs, where they are not stopped by the Roman wall, extend beyond the town limits to take in agricultural land. The meaning of this is that inasmuch as possession of a burghal tenement in the town carried with it rights in the agricultural land beyond the town, the area covered by the aggregation of these two connected holdings became the *territorium* of the legal corporation. In the other class of burghs the topographical aspect is different. There the extent of the *territorium* is not measured by the cultivated lands attached to the town, but by the girth of the old Roman wall enclosing in security a commercial community within. London is a good example of this. The Roman wall to this day is the boundary of the burghal limits, although there were citizens' lands beyond the wall, and, if I mistake not, burghal lands as well. But these extra mural lands did not come within the *territorium*—that was fixed by the ancient limits of the Roman wall.

Here then is the important contribution to the

principle of *locality* in local government. It did not come to London, York, Canterbury, Leicester, or Lincoln by charter or by Act of Parliament, but from the Roman civilization and power, which, though in the main swept away by Teutonic tribes and by Norman conquerors, still left the indestructible sites of *municipia* or *colonia* ; it did not come to the English burghs from charters or from law, but from the ancient system, older than charters or law, which belonged to the conquering Teutons in their tribal organization, and to the conquered British in their village organization.

A comparative study of the ancient ground-plans of the English and Scottish burghs well repays the careful student. He can pick out the examples of the two classes of burghs which I have just been dealing with, and he can bring to light many interesting and important points in the history of municipalities, gleaned, as is so often the case, not from meagre records, but from monumental remains, which speak so eloquently to those who know where to look for evidence.

Let me here summarize these somewhat intricate facts in the history of the burgh.

1. As far back as English records will take us we find the burghal town with the burgess organization, whatever that may have been.

2. The burgess tenement in the town was at once

the sign and the basis of the right of burgessship, and it carried with it rights to agricultural lands outside the town.

3. Burghs formed on purely English ground extended their boundaries to include both the town and town lands; burghs formed on ancient Roman sites cut short their boundaries at the town wall.

4. The ancient agricultural system of the village community applied to burghal towns as to open townships, and cultivation was carried on, subject to common rights and obligations.

5. Burghal tenements, though held originally in independent ownership, became in time subject to common rights incidental to burgessship.

6. The burghal community in its final development contained all the elements of the English village community, the burgesses being the equivalent of the free tribesmen at the top of the system, the agricultural villenage being at the bottom of the system.

7. Before coming within the province of English jurisprudence the burgh was a community of persons held together by common rights and common duties, and possessing common property in the agricultural land around them, which was the basis of their economical existence.

8. After coming within the province of English jurisprudence the burgh became a legal corporation.

As in the case of the counties, so then in the case

of the burghs, the point we have arrived at is that the *territorium* was not formed by an artificial aggregation of smaller units, but was an independent formation due to causes unconnected with the smaller units. The shire boundary fixed the boundary of the border townships within the shire, and the burgh boundary was just as absolute, for within the burgh there were no independent townships, but only wards and other convenient divisions for the government of the burgh. It is curious rather than significant, I think, that these internal divisions of the burgh are called by different names—they are shires in the city of York, hundreds in the burgh of Malmesbury, leets in the city of Norwich, wards in the city of London and elsewhere. It is true that in the boroughs, as elsewhere, the parish appears as a local division, but the parish in this case is not the equivalent, or practically the equivalent, of the township, as it is in the county outside the burghs. It is merely the ecclesiastical unit, having no connection whatever with municipal functions and work. Anybody looking at the map of the city of London, for instance, will see that the wards have no sort of relationship to the parishes, and, further, that the parishes are all named from the churches, and do not bear a second name derived from the old township—St. Michael, St. Anne, St. Faith's, etc., the simple ecclesiastical name; not St. Mary Abbots, Kensington; St. Mary, Islington

—the double name of ecclesiastical parish and civil township.

I now turn from this to another part of the subject. The "curia burgi," the "hustings court," the "burwaremote," the "portmote," or "portmanmote," are the names for the burgh assembly at different places. Like the ancient shire assemblies, the ancient burgh assemblies met in the open air. There are numerous instances of this, but perhaps the one that will appeal to you most is that of London, which met on a small plot of ground on the north side of St. Paul's, and is recorded in the Guildhall records as the land "*qui dicitur* folkmoot." The functions of the assembly are certainly diverse enough, and include so early as 1237, in the case of London, the making of a conduit to bring water to the city (*Mun. Gildhallæ*, ii. 66). It is not necessary to catalogue in detail all the functions which at one time or another, in one town or another, were performed by the burgh assembly or court. There are frequent cases of discontinuity of functions, frequent cases of the quiet assumption of new functions, frequent cases of the interference of the king to protect his ever-growing powers and assumed powers; but through it all the government of the borough in some sort and fashion has been absolutely continuous. So that, beginning with the conditions of a primitive community or with the independence derived from the Roman city, the burghs have brought their *territoria* and their system of self-government safely through all the political changes of a thousand years, and now stand at the bar of public opinion, performing many ancient functions of local government at the command of the State government, because of the maxim, "What the sovereign permits he commands," and many new functions of local government, because the sovereign has willingly utilized the old organization for the new duties.

You will remember that I quoted a legal definition of the county which showed the close connection between the *territorium* and the *communitas*—the locality and the community. The same definition applies to the burgh, and is even more closely suitable to the facts. The assembly of burghers sitting in session representing the whole community was the burgh; the whole community, the burgesses, were, until the Reform Act of 1835, the actual legal assembly of burghers without the machinery of representation, and this community of burghers was the burgh; the *territorium* consisting, in the English type of burgh, of burghal tenements in the town, and of the attached arable, pasture, and woodlands in the fields around the town, and, in the Roman type, of the wall-girt site of the ancient city—the *territorium* was the burgh. And in this intimate connection between *territorium* and *communitas* in the constitution of the county and of the burgh there lies the great principle of local government as it is revealed by natural development. That this intimate connection has been cut asunder by the legislation of later ages, when the meaning of county and burgh was scarcely understood, is a fact of some importance, for it has helped towards the indifference of citizens towards the burghal *territorium*, and towards the burghal *communitas*, and the concentration of all their attention upon the elected council of the burgh—as a thing apart from themselves, apart from the locality which it governs.

We have seen that the burgh and the township were closely allied. The burgh and the county were not in alliance. Every township that obtained burghal rank was a withdrawal from the jurisdiction of the shire or county, and the counties have not always submitted to this without a struggle. Thus in 1221 the vill, or township, of "Fairford, in Gloucestershire, claimed to behave like a borough, its men wanted 'to swear by themselves,' and the county of Gloucester testified against the claim—it had no warrant in practice" (Pollock and Maitland, *op. cit.*, i. 626). Exactly on all fours with this thirteenth-century case are two cases of only a few months old. The first is when the motion of Sir Albert Rollit, in the House of Commons, to allow certain boroughs below the rank of county boroughs to be endowed with the functions and powers of the Education measure of last session was carried in the House of Commons, and was immediately followed by the successful protests of the counties. But let us see how this is being followed up. The non-county boroughs are now combining, and the association of these boroughs for Lancashire, consisting of representatives of Ashton-under-Lyne, Bacup, Blackpool, Chorley, Colne, Darwen, Eccles, Haslingden, Heywood, Lancaster, Middleton, Nelson, Rawtenstall, Southport, Warrington, and Widnes, has issued a statement on the question as to what should be the educational authority in non-county boroughs for the purpose of providing technical and secondary education. The statement was unanimously approved at a meeting of the association, held on the 4th December, 1896, in Manchester. The statement urges the following points :—Prior to 1888 there was practically no distinction between boroughs, but all, great and small, had equal right of self-government accorded to them by their charters, and could not be controlled or interfered with by the county authority. The Act of 1888, by creating a distinction between boroughs above and below a population of 50,000, deprived the non-county boroughs of the safeguards they had up to that time possessed in being bound up by community of interests with the larger boroughs which had Parliamentary representation, and which, while protecting themselves, protected the smaller boroughs as well. The town council of a non-county borough is at present the educational authority upon whom rests the duty of providing technical instruction within its own area. The Government in 1890 granted the non-county boroughs' share, not to their town councils, but to the councils of the counties in which those boroughs are situate, exclusively and without imposing upon the county councils any obligation to pay or distribute the grant to the various local authorities within the administrative county, either according to rateable value or population, or both. It is pointed out that the best remedy would be the abolition of the arbitrary distinction created by the Local Government Act, 1888, between boroughs above and below a population of 50,000.

The second case is the struggle of the county of London against the city of London, a struggle which seeks to bring into the county jurisdiction the exempted area of the city, so that all London may share and share alike in respect of services that are of common benefit to the inhabitants of the whole area.

And thus with new aims and aspirations, with new motives and under new conditions, we have the old forms and the old relations of county and borough government.

IV

LOCALITIES (*continued*)—THE PARISH

THIRDLY, we have to consider, in connection with origins, the parish. I am compelled to use the term parish as the title of this section of the inquiry, because it is the only term known to local government for the lowest unit of administration. But it will not have escaped your attention that in discussing the county and the borough another term found its way into my vocabulary. This term was township; and when I tell you, or remind you—for you doubtless know the fact quite well already—that the parish is simply the township ecclesiastically considered, you will understand that I want now to go back to that older and better term for the purpose of discussing origins.

The going back to the old English term implies much more, however, than a mere academic preference for an English over a Greek word. For the thousand years or so during which it has been in use, the ecclesiastical, or parish, side of local government has considerably developed, while the civil, or township, side of local government has gone back. Thus in our own county of London, while the ancient civil parishes, or townships, of Islington, Camberwell, Lambeth, Chelsea, Kensington, Hampstead, and the rest, still remain, the ancient township (or city, as it became by charter) of Westminster through being cut up into ecclesiastical units, has caused the loss of Westminster from amongst London's choicest historical localities to obtain in its place St. Margaret's, St. John's, St. Clement's, St. Mary, St. James, and St. George Hanover Square. And when we reckon up the forces which make London interesting to Londoners and to others, the loss is not a small one.

Nor is the change from civil to ecclesiastical jurisdiction beneficial to local institutions throughout the country. I use the words of Sir Francis Palgrave to describe the situation as he learnt it in 1835, during the labours of the Municipal Corporation Commission:—

"A great deal of land was, and is, extra-parochial, but there is not an acre which is not in some township or ward, or at least in some ancient civil precinct of a similar nature, and hence a great deal of perplexity with respect to extra-parochial districts.

" Parishes are not so conveniently planned as the common law divisions. A township, or a ward, is usually a compact and well-rounded precinct; it was intended for the government of the people. The parish is very frequently irregular in its form, and composed of outlying or detached parcels, its boundaries having been determined by the possessions of the early patrons, whether laymen or ecclesiastical bodies, and, therefore, it is often quite unadapted for municipal purposes."

The history of the township, then, is what we have to consider in connection with the contribution it may be able to surrender to our inquiry. This history is lost in the unrecorded facts of the past, and we have to deal with the township as a *communitas*,—a legal unit which has not only duties, but also, as I think, rights,—and with the township in its undoubted connection with the manor. In the obscurity which thus surrounds the subject there are, as in the case of the burgh, the legal aspects of the case, and there are the historical aspects. Unfortunately, these do not agree, and the crusade against the idea of any archaic survivals occurring in our local institutions, in which our legal historians have done me the honour to single out my work for special attack, serves to widen the breach. This, of course, is not the place to discuss differences of opinion, so I must be content to state the case for my present purpose, with such knowledge and capacity as I possess, always bearing in mind, however, the check which legal scholars would impose upon other methods of enquiry.

I begin by pointing out a very important consideration—namely, that the initial element in the history of the township is, like that of the county and the burgh, in the *territorium*; but that, unlike the county and the burgh, the *territorium* of the parish is discoverable, not from historical, nor legal, nor economical evidence, but from geographical, or rather geological evidence. When the agricultural reformers of last century set to work to collect their information together, they found a certain well-defined system in the situation of the townships; and when geologists applied their science to the work of man on the earth's surface, they read the same well-defined system. Stripped of technical phrases, which are of no use to the present subject, and sometimes not correct, I will repeat the evidence which I collected in 1890 from two counties—Wiltshire and Sussex. In Wiltshire the valleys are, almost without exception, intersected longitudinally by rivulets, and are from three to five miles apart, hills intervening between them. The shape of the townships follows that of the valleys, and are, therefore, long, narrow strips from river to wood, with a right to the use of both. The farmers' houses were crowded together in villages situated on the banks of the stream, and the application of the land to each village was most uniform. The common meadows adjoined the river; next followed the arable, until the land became too steep or too thin to plough; then came the sheep and cow downs, and finally the woods at the extremity of the boundary, and adjoining the downs or woods of the townships in the opposite bourn.

Here, then, is evidence of systematic settlement, and I compare it with the south-east of England. There the chalk escarpment is the best marked physical feature. It is a steep-sided range of hills, having its summits remarkably level, and the ground falling gradually away with a slope from the crest. Mr. Topley, in examining this geological feature, was struck with the fact that the boundaries of the ancient townships followed exactly one plan so regularly as to afford undoubted evidence of "absolute facts which our forefathers have stamped on the great land divisions of the country." Everywhere along the foot of the chalk escarpment there is a line of villages. Everywhere the township ascends the escarpment, generally taking a good deal of the table-land above, occasionally ending off at or near the crest. Everywhere the villages are comparatively close together, and the townships consist of long, narrow strips, stretching from the valley up the side of the escarpment. Everywhere the homesteads are at the foot, where good water is to be found; the arable land adjoins; next comes the down land, to form the pasture ground; and the forest beyond completes the settlement.

Now here are neither political nor administrative

divisions of a country. The *territorium* is just that quantity and kind of land necessary for the support of communities independent of each other in all respects—communities supported by the produce of their lands and flocks, clothed from the wool and skins of their own herds, dependent upon their own laws and their own methods of punishment,—the stocks, the pillory, the tumbrel, and the whipping-post,—seeking wives and husbands from their own people, and looking upon neighbouring communities as foreigners, if not as enemies. Townships to this day in Scotland and the north of England look upon marriage outside the township community as hardly decent; refer to neighbours of other townships as foreigners; and, as in the case of Banbury, in Oxfordshire, up to 1803, possess no roads which indicated either the desire or need for intercommunication. I could, if time permitted, quote to you from the agricultural surveys of the end of last century example after example to show how late this interdependence of the townships lasted in this country.

Communities thus placed were more particularly identified with the *territorium* which held them than either the burgh or the shire. Like the burgh, therefore, and like the shire, the township is not a political division of the country, nor is it a division of the shire, or of the hundred, but it is a tract of territory formed to meet the common necessities of a community at a time when the country was a geographical, and not a political expression. This community and this territory has become the township of historical times—the parish, or lowest unit in the system of local government.

I will not repeat to you the detail of the primitive agricultural system which fitted into this ancient settlement, because I assume that Mr. Seebohm's book is well enough known to you; but when I remind you that its main feature is a group of villagers bound to each other by the close ties of common interests, perhaps of common blood; that these common interests were expressed in economical terms by the allotment of meadow and arable land every year in scattered bundles of acre-strips, so that each villager did not possess one single holding in severalty, but simply had the use of several long, narrow plots situated at different parts of the village lands, and which after the harvest were returned into common, again to be distributed the following year, in such a manner that each villager obtained for his use a different set of acre-strips each year; when I remind you, too, that the explanation afforded by this early system of economics has been alone able to account for some of the most remarkable phenomena of manorial custom and, be it added, of parish law and usage; when I point out that a great deal of this manorial and parish law has only been brought under the notice of lawyers and within the ken of the law courts by the fact that it frequently governed succession to property and rights in property; when I point out that even now the customary law of England has never been codified and placed on the same scientific footing as positive law; when I add that the main features of primitive village custom in England are repeated in France, Germany, and Scandinavia, in much the same relationship to modern law as they are found in England, while they are also repeated in Russia, Eastern Europe, and India, as the dominant, instead of the special, features of modern political organization—when these facts are duly weighed, I think you will agree with me that the English township is a factor in local institutions which must be approached, not from the modern aspect in which it is now found, but from the ancient aspect which began its history.

I am most anxious not to travel outside the immediate scope and object of these lectures, but I could not have got on without this preliminary explanation of the elements which go to make up the township.

After this stage the process is comparatively simple, because Bishop Stubbs becomes the chief guide. The corporate unity of the township was subjected to changes, both by way of development and under legislative action; but it is Sir Frederick Pollock who points out that, "although in the modern legal theory a parish or township is not capable of holding lands, yet lands belonging to a parish and administered by the churchwardens in aid of its other sources of revenue are frequently met with, so frequently, indeed, that the difficulties of legal title resulting from this state of things were brought to the attention of Parliament within the present century, and in one of the poor-law statutes (59 Geo. III. cap. 12, sec. 17, 1819) the churchwardens and overseers of any parish to which land belongs were incidentally made a body corporate for the purpose of dealing with it" (*Land Laws*, p. 38). I cannot help in passing referring back to what I have said about burghal incorporation, with a suggestion that the position of the parish with reference to legal incorporation in the nineteenth century is only a repetition of the position of the burgh in the fifteenth century.

Now the changes which Bishop Stubbs contemplates in the primitive township, before it comes into the light of history, shows it to have been broken up, as it were, into several bits—one bit had passed over to the lord, one to the manor, one to the church; and what remained was left in the hands of the civil parish as we now know it. But this cleavage, great though it was, was not accomplished without leaving recognisable scars upon the surface. Thus Bishop Stubbs admits that the primitive right of townsmen "to determine whether a new settler should be admitted to the township exists in the form of admitting a tenant at the court baron and customary court of every manor; the right of the markmen [townsmen] to determine the by-laws, the local arrangement for common husbandry, or the fencing of the hayfields, or the proportion of cattle to be turned into the common pasture, exists still in the manorial courts, and in the meetings of the townships; the very custom of relief and surrender, which are often regarded as distinctly feudal, are remnants of the polity of the time when every transfer of property required the witness of the community to whose membership the new tenant was thereby admitted" (*Const. Hist.*, i. 84, 85).

This is extremely important, but there is more to be added which our great constitutional historian has left unnoted. I turn to Sir Henry Maine for light upon the primitive characteristics of the law of distress, and for the significant note "that there is no more ancient institution in the country than the village pound; it is far older than the King's Bench, and probably older than the kingdom" (*Early Hist. of Inst.*, 203). Here, indeed, is the chief feature of a township system of law, which has not only come down to us by the right of making by-laws, as pointed out by Bishop Stubbs, and by the very etymology of the term "by-law" itself,—namely, the laws enacted by a township,—but by the survival of "by-law" men and "by-law" justice in its most primitive form. The Birlaw court, which appears in North England and Scotland, supplies the very evidence which Bishop Stubbs has noted is absent in the English township. "It is as an owner of land," he says, "not as a member of the community, that the freeman has rights and duties, and there is no evidence that in England the only way of owning land was the membership of the [mark] community" (*Const. Hist.*, i. 85). Now if we turn to the Birlaw court we find the evidence which is here stated to be wanting. Thus at Crawford, in Lanarkshire, the community consisted of the proprietors of land, called technically "freedoms." Each freedom was a bundle of acre-strips scattered over the *territorium* of the township. The Birlaw assembly, or court, was composed of all the owners of the freedoms, and they could not own freedoms without being resident members of the community. This court was held weekly, and determined the proportion and number of sheep, cows, and horses which the respective proprietors could keep on the commons, besides other business.

Here, then, is the ancient township in actual working order; and if we turn to another example —that of Whitsome, in Berwickshire—we can ascertain what the business of these Birlaw courts was beyond that of agricultural economics. In the first place, the Birlie men met upon a mound in the middle of the village, called the Birlie Knowe, and thither the villagers repaired to submit their grievances and obtain redress—in other words, their law was local law, and not sovereign law; their justice-court was the ancient township-moot, their judges were the townsmen.

I am sure I need not insist on the importance of such evidence as this. Outside the influence of the manorial element which entered so largely into the township life of Southern England, outside the influence of the seigniorial element which grew up with the Norman feudalism, outside the influence of Norman law and Norman sovereignty, but within the Teutonic area of settlement, the form of which was presented in the Wiltshire and Sussex evidence, we have in these cases untouched examples of the township organization as it first appeared upon the soil of Britain, when the only way of owning land was the membership of the community.

The township-moot, a word which occurs in a charter of Richard I., in its later development heard and adjudicated upon differences among the townsmen, contentious cases being carried to the hundred court; it elected its officers—the town-gerefa, or town-reeve, and beadle; it arranged the representation of its interests in the courts of the hundred and the shire, where the reeve and four best men appeared for the township; it carried out the requisitions of the higher courts in the way of taxes and other exactions, the pursuit of criminals and the search for stolen goods; and on the institution of frankpledge it prepared the lists for the view of the sheriff.

This view of the ancient township looms clearer out of the mists of the centuries than did that of the shire or the burgh, and when the further question is put as to how it is represented in modern facts, we have no difficulty in tracing the connection. "In the vestry meeting," says Bishop Stubbs, "the freemen of the township, the ratepayers, still assemble for purposes of local interest not involved in manorial jurisdiction; elect the parish officers, properly the township officers—the churchwardens, the waywardens, the assessors, and the overseers of the poor; while in the courts of the manor are transacted the other remaining portions of the township jurisdiction."

This much-abused parish meeting takes us back to the township, which was both *communitas* and *territorium*; and once again we have, therefore, the interlaced meaning of these two elements of local government. But in the parish this meaning is somewhat more significant. In the shire and in the burgh the *communitas* has come to be identified with the representative assembly, rather than with the whole body of shiremen, or burghers. The progress from the primary assembly, composed of the whole body attending personally, to the representative assembly, composed of selected individuals who act on behalf of the whole body, had been a gradual one until the principles of modern jurisprudence made representation the guiding principle of government. The open vestry was the last to succumb, for it is only by the provisions of the Act of 1894 that the elected parish council takes the place of the primary parish meeting for all practical purposes. The question is whether by substituting representation for personal attendance losses have not been incurred which it will be difficult to recover. Lord Coke, for instance, laid it down that the "inhabitants of a town without any custom may make ordinances or by-laws for the reparation of the church, or a highway, or *of any such thing which is for the general good of the public*, and in such case the greater part shall bind the whole without any custom" (5 Reports, p. 63A); and in a passage cited by Lord Coke from the year-book of 44 Edward III. (which is not yet published in the Rolls series), it is stated that "there is the usage through the length and breadth of the land for laws called by-laws—to wit, by assent of the neighbours—for raising money to make a bridge, or a causey, or sewer, and for assessing every man in a sum certain, and that they shall be able to distrain for this. . . . If such ordinance be made for a thing touching a probable common damage, the law as thus stated is beyond doubt. But if it be only for the advantage of individuals, none will be bound except those who have expressly assented."

The primary assembly of the township, therefore, had the right of taxation for a common benefit to the whole community; the subject of this common benefit was not limited by statutory definitions, of which modern law is so fond, but was left to be measured only by its effect upon the community; and I cannot but think that in this ancient township right there resides much of the evidence which lawyers are asking for as to the existence of common property, from which co-ownership is the legal outcome.

I do not know whether I have succeeded in bringing home to you that the ancient township, as it appears from the various sources of evidence to which I have directed attention, is something more than a merely loose assortment of neighbours living together for purposes of common agricultural privileges, or as co-tenants of one lord. What I have wished to do is to show that the *territorium* was fixed by the original settlers so as to contain all the means of independent economical existence; that the co-owners of this *territorium* were identical with the *communitas* of the township, and in that capacity alone determined questions of allotment of lands to individual user for every agricultural season, determined, too, other matters which made up the bundle of rights in the land inherent to each member of the community; that the co-owners in their capacity as a *communitas* adjudged disputes between individuals, and taxed for common purposes. But, having collected all these phenomena together, we still have to face the questions put by lawyers, with a reiteration which bespeaks a purpose. " Have we before us a *persona ficta*? or have we merely a group of co-owning individuals, brought together by reason of their co-owning rights?" Sir Frederick Pollock and Mr. Maitland answer this question by the statement that "what we see will tend to make us believe that it was much rather as a mere group of co-owning individuals than as a corporation that the members of the vill thought of themselves when they had a chance of applying either the one idea or the other. The manner in which the 'quasi corporateness' of the township was dissolved at the touch of law" is illustrated by many examples taken from the rolls of the Plantagenet period. But of these examples I would simply point out that they do not cover the entire ground. They neither reach the ground occupied by the Birlaw communities of Scotland, nor do they account for the modern touch of law which converted parishes into corporations just as readily as of old it dissolved corporations; still less does this legal evidence of the Plantagenet period reach back to the formation of the township *territorium*, which contained all the elements of economic independence, and which must have been formed by a group of persons possessing common interests and common rights in matters which could not have allowed the ownership of land to have escaped untouched. A manorial tenant was not only manorial tenant, he was township man as well. A manorial tenancy did not consist only of dues and services to the lord, but of rights and privileges in the manor which could be held against the lord. Examples occur, for instance, of a lord being fined for non-fulfilment of his duties (*Vill. Com.*, 117), and in one case—that of Pamber, in Hampshire—the lord was elected, not hereditary. Dues and services were not only dues and services to the lord, but to the community, for the "three days' work for the lord every week" is the correlation of the three days' right to employ himself on his own account which is found in more primitive groups than the English manor, as for instance in Ditmarsh. The course of events in England stamped the *work* days as the point to be translated into manorial law, the course of events in Ditmarsh stamped the *free* days as the point to be insisted upon as freemen's rights.

The township and the manor, then, together represent the ancient community, and the bundle of rights, duties, and powers which have come down with these divided jurisdictions are the rights, duties, and powers of *one communitas*.

I have, you will have noted, assumed the identification of the township and the parish, and there is no doubt, I think, that practically the identification is correct. In the north of England the ancient townships are very large, and the parish only occupies a portion of a township; in the south of England it sometimes happens that the townships are very small, and two or three go to make a single parish. But these idiosyncrasies do not destroy the general identification of township and parish. The township stands to the county as a unit to the whole. It has no such relationship to the borough, because, as we have already seen, the borough *is* the township specially organized. But this leaves open the position of the parish when not identical with the township—namely, parishes contained in the boroughs; besides which, I must deal with a still further matter brought into being by the Act of 1894.

The parishes contained in the boroughs are simply ecclesiastical districts, and nothing more—they are not townships from the ecclesiastical standpoint, they have never been townships, but are simple districts of the church, the " minster shire," the " priest shire," as they are called once or twice in ancient documents. This is an important distinction. The parishes of the city of York, or of the city of London, and other cities and boroughs, are known only by the name of the church to which they belong. In consequence of the poor-law legislation of Elizabeth's reign, these parishes shared in the new duties imposed upon parishes generally, and thus started a civil jurisdiction which they did not possess originally. Besides these there are, as in the modern county of London, ecclesiastical parishes—St. James Westminster, St. George Hanover Square, St. Clement Danes, and some others which were formed by special Acts of Parliament passed in the last century, and which became of civil importance by the Metropolis Management Act of 1855.

The effect of the Act of 1894 upon the parishes has left the subject in a very curious position. The parishes with over 300 population in all rural districts are to be governed by parish councils, the vestries and other authorities being abolished. This forms a special class of parishes with distinct functions of an important character, and with distinct legal relationship to district councils and to county councils. The parishes under 300 population are to be governed by a parish meeting, and they have distinct legal relationship to district councils and to county councils. Thus a second class of parishes are constituted. Again, the parishes in urban districts, and in boroughs, and in London are left untouched, with all their common law rights and their full organization, and thus form a third class of parishes. If these three classes of parishes had been formed for purposes of a definite nature, their position might be understood; but they have been formed by one of those accidents of legislation which have done more to place on the Statute Book false history and false evidence as to origins than any other source of historical errors, and which I cannot but think are not sufficiently studied by historians.

There is still another class of parishes to note, however—namely, the purely ecclesiastical parishes formed under the Act of 6 & 7 Vict. cap. xxxvii., for providing churches in populous places. These parishes have never varied from their original ecclesiastical purpose. They in no sense touch the institutions of local government, though units smaller than the parishes are necessary for various purposes of administrative supervision and control. These ecclesiastical districts might have been so constituted as to serve local government requirements as well as the ecclesiastical. They might well have assumed the old English name of tithing, with an elected headman, to be known as tithing-man. They are endowed by the census commissioners with all the dignity and importance of statistical units. But this position, valuable as it might be made, is now absolutely worthless, because of the indescribable ignorance of facts with which they have been constituted. Thus, to take the case of London, with which I am most familiar, but which is repeated all over the kingdom, we have the following state of things. These new parishes, formed, be it remembered, to meet the ecclesiastical requirements of a continuously populous area, and, therefore, capable of almost any arrangement in conformity with any reasonable requirements as to grouping, are arranged so that there are—

Ecclesiastical parishes or districts.		County of London.	City of London.
Conflicting with ancient parishes		61	2
Conflicting with County—			
Greater part inside ...	3		
Greater part outside ...	8		
	—	11	—
Conflicting with both County and City ...		—	2
Co-extensive with ancient parishes... ...		12	16
Not conflicting with, but forming parts of, ancient parishes		452	2
Constituted by grouping more than one ancient parish (of which eighty-nine in all are grouped)		—	34
Total ...		536	56
Reputed to be extra-parochial places for ecclesiastical purposes...		9	6

I have now dealt with the particular evidence to be derived from the historical side of local government. There remains to be considered one more point—namely, the comparative evidence. With the counties and the townships decaying in local government, with the hundreds dropping out of existence altogether, with the boroughs winning from the counties and from the State power after power during their battle for freedom, there is much to pause over and to question. Does this comparative evidence imply that the local government of the Anglo-Saxon system was inefficient and weak, and could not, therefore, stand the strain of the Norman sovereignty, and that the upgrowth of the boroughs in the fifteenth century is the true beginning of English local government? Does this particular side of the evidence introduce any new considerations as to the position of local government? If, as I have contended, we may definitely sweep away the highly organized and political system of the Romans as a factor in the origin of our institutions, and, therefore, with it the factor of an original servile, economical condition; and if we may look back upon an almost forgotten race for the beginning of things, with overflows of free Celtic tribesmen and free Teutonic tribesmen, to ultimately forge the primitive organization which received the shock of Norman sovereignty, we may fairly seek for economical changes to guide the last steps of progress. The legislation of Edward I. forms an epoch from which to date the decay of primitive local institutions. He laid the foundations of a system of national, instead of local, regulations for industry, and from that time forward the essentially local arrangements of manors and townships began to lose both their necessity and their utility. As Dr. Cunningham says, "In regard to commerce, manufactures, and to agriculture alike, the local authorities were gradually overtaken and superseded by the increasing activity of Parliament, till, in the time of Elizabeth, the work was practically finished" (*Industry and Commerce*, i. 243). We accordingly see the county and the parish almost lost as a part of the government machinery, and the borough, working towards its new position. Between the loss of primitive local institutions—counties with their tribal territories, burghs and townships with their communal territories—and the uprise of modern local institutions there existed a state of things which was neither "local" nor "government"; but all the same the facts of our history reveal the county, borough, and parish as the true forms of English local government which have survived the stress of centuries. These ancient areas, formed by early communities possessing the strongest of common interests, have never been released from the ties of common interests. These common interests have governed the relationship of property in respect of its economical value for centuries; they have formed the principle of taxation for common purposes; they have established that *locality* in local government is not a mere legislative creation but an unconscious development of forces which belong to the national existence. The county locality, the borough locality, the parish locality, are all alike built out of material which comes from the common interests of self-formed communities.

I have left it for this stage to say a few words about the mischievous and absurd misuse of the names of the ancient localities of the country by Government departments in order to express some statistical or administrative fact. Thus we have the ancient county, the administrative county, the registration county; we have the parish and the district.

The difference between the ancient county and the modern administrative county does not need the introduction of a new term. The former has ceased to be of any constitutional value, and might, for all purposes except that of history, be ignored. The registration county is an absurdity only possible, I should think, to English methods of government—a relic of the system when local government was synonymous with poor law. Finally, there are the parish and the district. In many cases, as I have already explained, these two areas are identical; and even where they are not so there is no object in keeping up the old parish area. A parish which has developed into a "district," and a group of parishes which has been formed into a "district," are distinct entities bearing definite relationship to the local government system of the country. They should be so, then, for all local purposes, and they could well assume the old English title of *town* for urban, and *township* for rural communities.

K

V

THE FUNCTIONS OF LOCAL GOVERNMENT

THE task before me now assumes a different aspect altogether to that presented by the preceding lectures. I have to discuss the problems of local government according to modern requirements, and to some extent according to modern procedure; and I have to gather the elements which make up these problems partly from the ancient facts already dealt with, partly from modern facts not yet dealt with.

The ancient facts already dealt with have, I hope, produced the impression of certain principles being at work in the minds of our forefathers—principles that did not depend upon philosophers and schoolmen, principles that were the unconscious product of all sorts of forces—economical, political, physical, and religious—in the minds of early races. The modern facts to be dealt with are governed by principles which are the conscious products of definite study by philosophers and schoolmen, and of definite aims by politicians and capitalists.

I want to set out upon the extremely difficult task now before me with a clear understanding of the elements which present themselves for discussion, and I shall first endeavour to define these elements.

There are, first, the ancient undestroyed elements. The whole area of the country is occupied by localities formed in very ancient times, or upon the model and upon the same principle of very ancient times. These localities are the counties formed from the tribal organization, the boroughs formed from the primitive industrial organization, the townships formed from the primitive agricultural organization; all three—counties, boroughs, and townships—being, therefore, formed principally upon an economical basis. Originally formed by communities whose settled political and religious ideas compelled them towards independence, the development of property within these localities has been governed for long centuries by the common rights and the common burdens belonging to each locality. Property has descended by family succession; has been transferred from one ownership to another; in later years has been bought and sold, subject to a solid weight of economical influences which have inured owners to the conception of common interests, rights, and duties within the sphere of these early formed localities. I have already pointed out how the legislation of Edward I.

began the process of substituting a national system of economics for the old local system, and I quoted Mr. Cunningham's opinion that the process was not completed until Tudor times. In its strictest sense, however, the process cannot be said to be completed even yet. It is true that all the important food products, all the important industries, all the great movements of commercial enterprise are now freed from local influences, and are getting to be free from many national influences; but the economical local influences cannot be said to have ceased so long as ancient manorial dues, rights, and privileges continue to exist, so long as ancient tithes are levied, so long as the land tax is unredeemed, and so long as the law of primogeniture governs succession to property as well as to title.

Now I simply point out to you the splendid machinery which the ancient localities provide for a system of local government. Occupying the entire area of the country, formed originally for actual and complete independence, bringing down with them to modern times property so economically interlaced with property that even sentiment demands that the area of common burdens shall be identical with the area of inherited common interests, looking back upon a history often recorded in the parish church and the parish burial-ground, and often enshrined in the annals and traditions of family life, we have presented to us a map of the country covered with self-grown localities of the most perfect type.

Secondly, there are the elements derived from modern requirements. To rightly understand these we should consider the functions of government administered by local authorities during the period from the reign of Edward I. up to the fifteenth century, when the State interfered very slightly in the internal affairs of localities; the functions of government created by legislation since Tudor times, and which were administered in the manner provided by the State without regard, or without much regard, to the local authorities which existed or were growing into power; and the functions of government demanded by modern requirements, the subject of modern scientific and philosophical thought, affected by modern economical conditions and claims.

I do not attempt to hide the complicated nature of these two classes of phenomena and the difficulties in the way of co-ordination and definition. What appears to be abundantly clear is that the genius of our race has supplied modern times with definite localities contained within the area of the country, and that it falls upon the modern enquirer to ascertain what functions of government should be granted to these localities, and what should be the principles which should guide the legislator in allotting these functions.

At this point I am assisted by the doctrine of general utility, which the great genius of David Hume, and perhaps the greater genius of Jeremy Bentham, have formulated for us. I will venture to quote the definition, although it is doubtless well known to most of you, because it is well for all of us who are dealing with certain definite ideas and conceptions to have before us exact terminology, and not a terminology dependent upon memory or upon association. The definition of general utility which I choose as the best is that contained in the opening words of Bentham's treatise on the *Theory of Legislation*: "The public good ought to be the object of the legislator; general utility ought to be the foundation of his reasonings. To know the true good of the community is what constitutes the science of legislation; the art consists in finding the means to realize that good." Great and simple words are these, and they will guide us through many of the difficulties of the subject.

These difficulties begin to appear when an attempt is made to define or to ascertain the material for obtaining a definition of the proper functions of local government. It is quite easy to say, and would satisfy some people, that the proper functions of local government are just those functions of government which are as a matter of fact imposed upon or granted to localities by the State. But, of course, this only avoids the real question, and does not answer it, because there is the anterior question—what functions should the State take over to itself, and what should it leave to the private individual? Now in no case that I know of has the State consciously discussed the advisability or necessity of removing from the domain of private action any given function before it has handed it over to or imposed it upon local government. There is no distinction in modern legislation between the act of declaring a function to belong to the sphere of government and the act of imposing or conferring it upon local governments. No doubt some sort of preparation and preliminary consideration is given by individual ministers or individual legislators to the question as to whether a certain function is proper to be taken over by government. It was so in the case of elementary education, it was so to a less extent in the case of light railways, it has been so to some extent in the case of secondary education. But these subjects have formed what are called "burning" questions of the day, and being of considerable magnitude in their operation and effect upon ratepayers and upon other interests, they get discussed in a more or less informal manner. But side by side with the informal character of the discussion relating to such subjects as these are many other subjects which are scarcely discussed at all, and I may mention the case of electric-lighting as an example. And surely the anomalous position of water supply is another example. Left entirely to the initiation of local authorities themselves, the function of water supply has never been placed by the Government in a position such as light railways are placed, or such as electric-lighting and tramways are placed. And yet surely water supply is far more necessary to localities than either of these other services. What, then, with the informal character of the discussion as to the propriety or otherwise of creating a new function when discussion takes place at all, and what with the entire absence of discussion on principle, I come back again to my statement that the act of creating a new function of local government is never preceded by any conscious act of declaration that such a function is proper to be transferred from the sphere of private action to that of government control. We cannot, therefore, be satisfied with the general proposition that the proper functions of local government are just those functions of government which the State determines to hand over to subordinate local governments.

We must, therefore, grapple more closely with the question as to what may be said to be the functions proper to local government. As a general conception of the definition, the functions proper to local government may be said to consist of those functions properly under Government control, and which, on account of their local interests and value, and of the limited range of benefits conferred by them, are best administered by or entrusted to local governments.

The point of this definition is the word "properly," and it clearly imposes upon us the necessity of enquiry into the proper functions of government. Of course, as you all know, the functions of government have been discussed from the earliest times of philosophical writing, and the great name of Plato, and still greater of Aristotle, at once occur to the mind. But it is impossible to range over the enormous literature of this subject, and I am anxious to get directly to that part of the subject relating to local government. For this purpose I must accept some of the most important conclusions of those recognised authorities who have examined into this question. There are three schools. The *laisser-faire* school, consists of those who would relieve Government of everything, and of those who would relieve Government of all functions except a few that by long association and practice are looked upon as absolutely necessary or convenient; the socialistic school, consists of those who would place upon Government every function now left to private action, and of those who would place upon Government a large proportion of functions now left to private action. Between these two the range of choice is clearly very wide, but there is an intermediate school also which has a definite range, and I shall call this the economical school.

For our guidance to the conclusions of the economical school we have the great name of John Stuart Mill, and I would still venture to recommend the study of his chapter on "the limits of the province of Government." It is not quite conclusive, it is disfigured by one or two hasty conclusions and by one or two illustrations which will not bear analysis, it implies at one stage much more than is really meant when later sections are studied, and it is deficient in historical evidence. But, drawbacks as these undoubtedly are, it is a very valuable summary from the economical standpoint, and sadly wants filling out by competent scholars.

When Mr. Mill sums up his case by the remark that "letting alone should be the general practice : every departure from it, unless required by some great good, is a certain evil," he has clearly in his mind those disastrous and iniquitous proceedings of the old government of France which have been described by M. Dunoyer. Setting out with the general proposition that "as a general rule the business of life is better performed when those who have an immediate interest in it are left to take their own course," Mr. Mill proceeds to enquire into those cases where the interest and judgment of the consumer or person served are not sufficient security for the goodness of the commodity he is provided with, and he instances education, the over-working of children, poor-relief, lunacy, colonization, the accumulation of knowledge and data for scientific use, and other subjects which do not belong to our immediate purpose. But in selecting or instancing these cases Mr. Mill makes a remarkable inclusion which I must quote in his own words: "Whatever if left to spontaneous agency can only be done by joint-stock associations will often be as well and sometimes better done, as far as the actual work is concerned, by the State. . . . I have already more than once adverted to the case of the gas and water companies, among which, though perfect freedom is allowed to competition, none really takes place, and practically they are found to be even more irresponsible and unapproachable by individual complaints than the Government. . . . In the case of these particular services the reasons preponderate in favour of their being performed like the paving and cleansing of the streets—not certainly by the general government of the State, but by the municipal authorities of the town. . . . But in the many analogous cases which it is best to resign to voluntary agency the community needs some other security for the fit performance of the service than the interest of the managers, and it is the part of Government either to subject the business to reasonable conditions for the general advantage or to retain such power over it that the profits of the monopoly may at least be obtained for the public. This applies to the case of a road, a canal, or a railway."

Let me note in passing how this passage illustrates once more that no great authority, like Austin, or Bentham, or Mill, has thought fit to determine the principles of local government as distinct from the principles of government in general. It goes very far, indeed, on economical grounds towards enlarging the province of local government to administer or control, or to itself make and use the profits, or to tax the profits of all services of general utility which are monopolies, and not subject to the free influences of competition; and I will say at once that I shall make no such claim as this.

I do not think these propositions, valuable as they are as guides, are sufficient as definitions of the proper functions of local government. They give us three important data—namely, that the functions of government should include

(1) Services where the interest and judgment of the consumer are not sufficient to secure the goodness of the commodity.

(2) Services which must be performed by the agency of a joint-stock company.

(3) Services whose due performance is necessary in

the public interest, but cannot be attained by being left to the uncontrolled interests of private financial managers.

But there are other data which seem to me to be also as necessary as these. Thus the services proper to become functions of local government must be those of elemental necessity or convenience, must be in the nature of monopolies, or freed from all the general conditions of competition, must be services which to be carried on will interfere with one or more of the general rights of the community, must be complementary or supplementary to the other services of local government, must be for public as well as for private use and benefit, and must in a general sense be paid for by some system of taxation, direct or indirect, or, if paid for according to services rendered, must be at such a charge as to render the service available to the poorest class of the community. This may appear to be a formidable list of conditions to attach to a service before it can be allowed as a proper function of local government, but there are some services which answer to all these conditions, and yet are not universally functions of local government; and there are some services which do *not* answer to all, and yet are, nevertheless, functions of local government. The fact is that these conditions are not intended to be applied to every case in their entirety, nor is it necessary that they should be so applied. They constitute together the supreme standard by which in all reason the functions of local government may be judged, but to which all functions imposed upon local government cannot attain — a standard which should be used as a measurer, and not as a conforming test.

Taken in their broadest sense, these definitions of the functions of local government might include many services of general utility which are now by common consent of all practical people left entirely in the hands of private enterprise. Let me refer to the supply of bread, quoted only quite recently by Sir John Lubbock in this connection. This is a service of general utility to all the community alike, and it happens that in the past it has been one of the functions of local government. In the fifteenth and sixteenth centuries the proper provision of corn for the citizens was one of the common trading enterprises of the towns (Ashley, *Economic History*, ii. 36); while, according to the theory which still held its ground in the sixteenth century, that "victual, being a necessary sustenance for the body, should not be esteemed at the seller's liberty," a fixed price was set on all provisions (Mrs. Green, *Town Life*, ii. 36). Hence the Assize of Bread and the close watching of victuallers, lest in selling meat, eggs, butter, or oatmeal, they should take "excess lucor upon them, selling, that is to say, more than 1*d.* in the 12*d.*" (*Hist. MSS. Com.*, ix. (1) 288).

Mrs. Green, in her valuable and interesting work on *Town Life in the Fifteenth Century* (ii. 36–40), has quoted instance after instance from the municipal records showing the steps taken by the mediæval borough to keep in the hands of the community the supply of food, and the modern regulations as to adulteration, as to weights and measures, as to bakehouses, and as to markets, show that the entire element has not dropped out of the functions of local government. But, of course, food supply is not now a local concern at all. At one time in our history, when each village community was economically an independent unit, it was essentially a local concern, and was under the control of local authorities. But, fortunately, the growth of food stuffs and the distribution of food has passed out of the range of local interests, and has become national. The growth of foreign commerce in food material, the conditions of protection and free trade, the movements of capital no longer attached to a locality nor even to a nation, have definitely settled that the local conditions of Scotland in the last century, of Oxfordshire, as at Banbury, in the seventeenth century, of England altogether in mediæval times, in respect of food products have altogether passed away, and with them the possibility of those terrible local famines of which there are records in our own history, and from which India, for the same causes, is now suffering.

But if food supply has passed out of the sphere of local government, it is well to point out that one special section of it—namely, agricultural produce—has not altogether passed out of the sphere of the State government. In 1796 the Lord Mayor of the city of London, "owing to the extreme dearness of provisions, particularly bread, which bears so hard on the lower classes of society, withstood the combination of a few monopolizing individuals to keep up the price of flour beyond its fair average with the value of wheat. The latter part of the mayoralty was a scene of contention between the public duty of the magistrate and the contrivances of the mealfactors. The Lord Mayor introduced a bill for the *erection of public grinding mills* to remedy the inconvenience so much complained of" (*Times*, 9th November, 1796). While just a century later, 1896, the Government of the country carry a measure through Parliament which applies Imperial taxation to the support of agricultural industry—a measure whose only justification is founded upon the principle that the supply of corn for bread is a function of government.

But I mention these facts only to dispose of the element of communal trading which they introduce into the elements of local government. The economical laws of free competition govern these cases now, and will continue to govern them so long as society is framed upon the present commercial basis. It is not within the province of local government to enter into competition with the private trader, unless and until private trade is abolished,—a contingency not to be at present considered, and not, as I think, very likely to be considered in the future,—or unless and until private trade ceases to perform its legitimate functions. This is not so remote a contingency. In three cases, at all events, it comes perilously near to this neglect. In one case—that of pawnbroking—not only has the State been compelled in our own country to enter upon the domain of private industry and establish laws for the protection of the consumer, but in France, Switzerland, and other countries the State has actually taken over the function of pawnbroking as a duty of local government. The second case to which I have thought it advisable to allude is still, so far as I know, in the hands of private enterprise, uncontrolled by the State. It is that of coal supply. Competition in this case no doubt regulates prices fairly enough when the consumer can afford to purchase in sufficient quantities; but not only are there signs that the protection afforded by competition may not always be secured to the general body of consumers, but in the case of the poor, who can only purchase in very small quantities, competition does very little, for the price at which they are compelled to purchase this first necessity of tolerable existence is out of all proportion to the current market price; and it is a question whether the municipality should not be compelled to provide coal for sale in small quantities at prices regulated by the current market price. The third case where either the State or local government may properly cross the line which divides private industrial enterprise from the functions of government is the sale of alcoholic liquors upon the now well-known Gothenburg system. All these cases come under that condition formulated by Mill as to the services which should come under government control—namely, those services whose due performance is necessary in the public interest, but cannot be attained by being left to the uncontrolled interests of private financial managers.

You will no doubt have observed that in discussing the terms of the definition of the proper functions of local government I used a phrase of some significance, a phrase which opens up some very important considerations. I spoke of functions of government as withdrawals from the sphere of private action, and it is very important to bear this in mind, for it raises the question, When and where does it become right and advisable to withdraw from the sphere of private action certain functions of life and transfer them to government control? This question is being discussed now in a fashion that brings into prominence the passions of party conflicts, and it happens that the battle rages round the term "socialism," with which are associated all sorts of ideas with which local government has nothing whatever to do, and which in no way influence its functions. To the minds of some people it is sufficient to call a thing socialism—rank socialism is, I believe, the full expression—to condemn, not only the thing, but the person advocating or dealing with it, to the depths of iniquity. But those of us who discuss the problems of life upon scientific lines get used in time to the epithets of ignorant passion, and then the term socialism has no longer any terrors.

Nevertheless, it is a pity that this term has become a word in the vocabulary of politics, and especially is it a pity that in connection with the question as to when and where private action should give place to government control it is most freely used. I do not think you are in danger of hearing much socialism from me, but it is, unfortunately, necessary to warn you against the unhappy associations of this portion of our enquiry in order not to allow a subject, which should be free from all bias of passion, to be dragged on one side by false interpretations.

Now the significance of the statement that every new function of government is a withdrawal from the sphere of private action rests upon a very prevalent assumption that private action has the first claim.

This assumption is due to the teaching of the political economists, and is not due to historical fact. If I were making a claim for government control, and especially local government control, I should travel back to the period of village communities, to the period in English history represented by the conditions of modern Russia or modern India, and I should point out that the evidence of this period and of the economic evolution which has taken place since this period all goes to make it clear that every exercise of private action is, in fact, a withdrawal from the sphere of local government. It is no bar to this conclusion that the subject-matters which attract private enterprise and which are under government control in modern times are not the same subject-matters which were under the control of the village communities of prehistoric times, because industrial and economical enterprise and necessities have descended by gradual stages from prehistoric times just as institutions have descended.

What I am anxious to convey to your minds is that we have two distinct pieces of evidence on this subject : the economical evidence that every new function imposed upon or granted to local government is a withdrawal from the sphere of private action; and the historical evidence that every function undertaken by private enterprise is a withdrawal from the sphere of local government. When, therefore, adopting the economical standard, as I do adopt it, because it is founded upon the doctrine of general utility, I have to ask the question, When and where does it become right and proper to withdraw from the sphere of private action certain functions of life and transfer them to the control of local government? I hold myself free to discuss it untrammelled by any such assumption as generally prevails that because private enterprise has economically the first claim upon all industrial undertakings it has, therefore, an absolute claim for all time upon all undertakings which may bring profit to individual enterprise.

Even dismissing all ideas of communal trading, it is clear, according to the standard I have previously laid down, that the functions of local government must penetrate into the domain which private capital has, especially during late years, urgently claimed as its own by some sort of inherent right, which, however, has never been properly defined. Before proceeding further I must shortly examine this side of the question, because when once it is clearly understood many of the difficulties of the problem will be cleared away; for I do not think it too much to affirm that the consideration as to what functions should be allowed to remain under, or be transferred to, the control of local government, has hitherto depended much more upon the demands of private capitalists than upon questions of principle; and thus matters of great moment are left for settlement, not upon calm consideration of all the facts from the point of view of local government, but in the battle ground of public and private interests. And yet what are the facts? Three hundred years ago private capital was not plentiful, and it was difficult, if not impossible, to raise money for purposes now held to be among the rights of private capital to undertake. There was no fire insurance at the time of the Fire of London, and the Corporation of the City of London were among the first to commence municipal insurance. The complaints of townspeople of the decay of their ancient roadsteads and harbours were numerous and bitter; rivers required deepening and straightening; docks required establishing and maintaining; water supply needed organizing and constructing. But for all these subjects private capital was not forthcoming, and local authorities were left alone to accomplish the work, and nothing was heard of the claims of private capital to undertake all and everything that would bring in sufficient profit.

Let me give a few instances. More than three hundred years ago tonnage rates on shipping were allowed to be levied for the improvement of Dover harbour (23 Eliz. cap. 6). The Corporation of London stand out honourably first in undertaking, in 1571, as a municipal necessity "such a convenient and meet cut as may serve for navigation" of the river Lea;

and at Chichester the mayor and citizens obtained powers to cut out, trench, and draw the haven to the city suburbs. Grants of similar powers lead on to a long course of improvements in the navigation of rivers, began under James I., but chiefly carried out after the Restoration. Municipal authorities were the first to benefit trade by spending upon harbour or river improvements such money as they could command from their corporate property, or as could be raised upon the security of their scanty rating powers. In Liverpool, the corporation, in 1709, gave for the construction of a convenient wet dock or basin four acres of land, parcel of the waste belonging to them, but as the proposed works would "cost more than the inhabitants and corporation can raise," they procured an Act authorizing them for twenty-one years to charge rates on shipping entering the port (8 Anne, cap. 12). In matters of water supply, Gloucester appears to have been first to take the matter up as a municipal necessity. There were ancient conduits conveying water to the city, probably the successors of Roman conduits to this ancient Roman city. In 1541-42 these had decayed, and the Mayor and Dean of Gloucester were in that year authorized jointly to renew them and dig for springs (35 Henry VIII. cap. 10). Two years afterwards the Corporation of London obtained similar powers, but in 1613 the powers of the Corporation were transferred to Sir Hugh Myddleton, and thus London lost this valuable prerogative. "Municipal authorities, therefore," to use the words of Mr. Clifford, in his *History of Private Bill Legislation* (i. 10), "who have in recent years taken over the water service from private companies have only returned to their old ways."

Now the necessities which caused such functions as these to be recognised as municipal functions three hundred years ago are not altered by the lapse of time. They are public necessities still, and could not under any circumstances be allowed to become circumscribed by the limited duty which private capital assumes to itself—namely, the duty simply of providing a sufficient amount of income to pay dividends. I am aware, of course, that this duty carries with it the necessity for a certain amount of efficiency and a certain amount of stability. But because, on the one hand, the interests of private capital have become so strong and the powers of municipalities have become so weak, the principle lying at the root of the matter has been allowed to drop out of cognizance, and all sorts of views antagonistic to the principles of local government, if not subversive of local government altogether, have become rife, and in some instances dominant.

Much misconception, for instance, exists as to certain municipal services which are held to be "remunerative services"—that is, services worked at a profit, which profit goes to the relief of the general ratepayer, and not to the credit of private capital. I myself have considerable sympathy with private capital in every true case of profitable competitive trading, but I must insist upon the definition of *profit* being correct. In many, if not in all, cases where this question is seriously raised in this country at the present moment, the only criterion of the so-called profit is that in the hands of private owners these services are made to pay dividends on private capital. But any municipal service can be made to pay dividends on private capital, if only the means of levying a revenue are granted to private owners; and the true criterion of profit in these cases is not, therefore, the power of private capital to earn dividends, but the means by which private owners are allowed to collect revenue. If the revenue collected by private owners is some form of taxation, of course all question of profit ceases; only if the revenue is in repayment of services does the question of profit appear, and then only under some conditions.

Thus if the services paid for by the consumer in proportion to use or consumption are such that every inhabitant is bound by necessity, by the requirements of the law, or by an option so generally put into force that it scarcely amounts to option, to avail himself of these services, the revenue collected by such means cannot be distinguished from taxation; nay, it is taxation—the old system of taxation according to benefit, instead of the modern system, according "to a fair and equal pound rate," as the statute puts it.

Most people would agree that rights of taxation should reside only in the taxpayers, and it is by this principle that the claims of private capital can best be tested. The right of taxation is under the present system exercised by private owners in each of its three forms—namely, direct taxation, indirect taxation, and taxation according to benefit, and I will give a few examples of these taken only from the services which are recognised functions of local government.

Water supply is for two purposes—house sanitation and domestic use. The first can only be met by direct taxation, just as all other charges for sanitation; the second might be met by a charge according to consumption, but the difficulties are so great that taxation is generally resorted to. In the case of docks, harbours, and markets the cost is met by dues, tolls, and rents upon shipping or upon produce, in other words by indirect taxation. In the remarkable case of the Deptford cattle-market, the Corporation of the City really stand in the position of private owner. They are not properly the local authority, but they were allowed to establish the market "without having recourse to the imposition of rates for the purpose, other than what may be derived from the tolls of the market itself"—that is to say, they substituted indirect for direct taxation. In the case of cemeteries the cost is met primarily by taxation according to benefit, the deficiency, if any, falling upon direct taxation; while the cost of burying persons whose property is not able to meet the specialized charge is borne wholly upon direct taxation. In some cases a surplus over and above the cost is levied and applied to the relief of direct taxes, and in this case the surplus so charged is clearly indirect taxation. In the case of gas, electric-lighting, baths and wash-houses, tramways and telephones, so long as the entire cost is met by the charges for services, and so long as the charges for services are only sufficient to meet the cost, the taxation is according to benefit. But when either the charges for services are not sufficient to meet the cost, and the deficiency has to be met out of taxation (as is often the case with baths and wash-houses), or when the charges for services are more than sufficient to meet the cost, and the surplus is applied to relieve direct taxation (as is the case with tramways), the element of both direct and indirect taxation appears. In the first case the deficiency is an extra charge upon direct taxation; in the second case the surplus is indirect taxation—*i.e.*, a charge, over and above the cost, upon each of the persons using the services.

The distinction between these services is, therefore, that in some cases the whole cost is met by direct or indirect taxation, in other cases the first cost is met by taxation according to benefit, while a deficiency in the first cost falls upon direct taxation, and a surplus derived from the first cost is indirect taxation of the consumer or user of the services.

My analysis of the different kinds of taxation in the case of services, partly municipal and partly in the hands of private owners, will, I hope, have destroyed the partition wall that is sometimes attempted to be erected between different kinds of services, and which is built up of false economical conceptions. It also establishes that the primary test of whether a particular service is properly a function of local government depends, not upon whether it can be made remunerative to private capital, but upon whether it is a service of such general utility that its inefficiency or abandonment would cause damage to the community. No locality can afford to allow water supply, markets, cemeteries, fire insurance, lighting, locomotion, drainage, sanitation, education, fire protection, to be absolutely non-existent, and in most localities it is essential that these services be efficient in a high degree; certain localities, like Liverpool, Glasgow, Bristol, Southampton, and other ports, cannot afford to allow their docks and harbours to remain undeveloped or to get into bad condition. And so on of other services. And thus the general demands of a community, or the general necessities of a community, constitute the first ground for defining a given service as a proper function of local government.

Services which are of general utility, which are compulsory, or which are generally demanded in the interests of a locality, are met, as I have shown, by some form of taxation, namely :—

(1) According to benefit.

(2) Indirectly upon the consumer.

(3) Directly upon assessed rates.

(4) Partly according to benefit, and partly indirectly upon the consumer.

(5) Partly according to benefit, and partly directly upon assessed rates.

This view of the relation of these services to taxation is very important. It has, I think, been wholly missed hitherto. The keynote to its explanation is the compulsory nature of the service—compulsory from necessity, compulsory by law, compulsory from demands of the community. Private capital will only supply such services if it is allowed to be profitable. So soon as profit ceases private capital ceases to supply the service. Therefore the matter is left in this position. Private capital wishes to reap benefit from the necessities of the community, but will not share loss. It demands a higher rate of interest than capital in the hands of public authorities. It does not necessarily command higher efficiency in production when the commodity produced is not subject to the laws of choice and competition.

I want further to explain the principle of taxation according to benefit, and I will examine more closely those services which illustrate this principle.

I commence with two services which have undergone a change from taxation according to benefit to taxation according to an equal rating, or which exhibit other important illustrations of this part of the subject.

The sanitary laws have made it compulsory to clear away all refuse from houses or other premises. Formerly this was a matter of individual choice. Thirty years ago it would have been undertaken by private enterprise, because it was remunerative. House refuse was of value for brick-making and other industries, just as stable refuse is still of value. But before private capital could step in the removal of house refuse was constituted a function of local government, and for a long time the sanitary authorities obtained large sums from private capitalists for the permission to collect house refuse. Then the brick industry changed and sanitary science became more exacting, until now the same service is a heavy charge upon the ratepayers—not according to benefit, but according to equal rating. On the other hand, the removal of stable refuse is still a private function and a profitable one, but it is under the control and inspection of the sanitary authority, the cost of such control and inspection being paid, not by owners of stables, but by the general ratepayer. I do not here raise the important question of the economics of waste products, which in America is being properly studied, but I point out the change in one service from a condition of profit to private capital to a condition of loss, and the withdrawal of private capital from the service, leaving the loss to fall upon the community.

Another interesting case of transition is that of elementary education. The State has since 1870 declared this to be compulsory, but it has left a large element of choice to each individual. But, over and above the choice as to private education, there is the compulsory public education. This was originally met partly by school-pence, as the parents' weekly payment was called, and partly by equal taxation—that is to say, the cost of this service was met by taxation partly according to benefit and partly by equal taxation. But the abolition of the school-pence in 1891 caused the taxation according to benefit to cease, and in its place was substituted equal taxation. The same cost is incurred by the local authority now as was incurred before 1891, but its incidence is shifted; and my point is, that if it is taxation now, it was taxation before 1891, the conditions as to cost incurred being absolutely the same.

I now pass on to examples of services met by mixed systems of taxation and I will take the case of cemeteries. Every inhabitant is bound at death to be buried or cremated; the community is bound to see that the disposal of the dead is properly carried out. Therefore, although the fees for burial are collected according to the services rendered,—that is, there is choice as to place and mode of interment,—the fees so paid are taxes, and—whether the cemetery is in the hands of the State, as in the singular and unfair case of West Brompton Cemetery, in London, or in the hands of local authorities, as in the case of many districts in London and the country, or in the hands of private owners, as in the case of Woking, Kensal Green, and other places—the revenue collected is taxation, and there is no question of profit — no question of the service being a remunerative service. What actually happens is that the State or local government either collects, by way of burial fees, too little revenue to cover the cost of administration,—in which case the cost is met partly by taxation according to benefit, and partly by direct taxation on assessed rates,—or the State or local government collects more revenue than is necessary to cover the cost of administration; in which case the cost is met wholly by taxation according to benefit, beyond which there is imposed further taxation upon the payers of burial fees—that is, indirect taxation of the consumer, which is applied to the benefit of the direct taxpayer. In neither case is it a question of "profit and loss" by competitive or monopoly trading; it is a mere method of raising the money necessary to meet a compulsory service to the community; and because human vanity and the immensely strong force of traditional respect for dead ancestors enables the local authority to impose a specialized tax according to the old principle of benefit, and not according to the modern principle of "a just and equal pound rate," it does not convert a burial fee into something which is not taxation. The compulsory nature of the service is the ruling factor in the matter, and the test of this compulsory nature is in those cases where, by reason of poverty or by reason of ignorance of the personality of the body, as in the case of the drowned, the cost of burial is not met by specialized charges, but by direct taxation.

When the function of providing burial-grounds is in the hands of private capital, the nature of the burial fee as a specialized tax is not altered. What has happened is that private capital has been allowed to repay itself out of the proceeds of taxation.

I lay some stress upon this example, because I

apprehend there will be less in dispute in the case of burial-grounds than in some other examples of this class of service. It is a common-law right that every person may be buried in the churchyard of his parish where he dies without paying anything for breaking the soil, and a small treatise published by Sir Henry Spelman in 1641, *De Sepulturâ*, is still worth reading in this connection. That this common-law right was first infringed upon by the clergy after the reformation in their uncanonical exaction of burial fees, that it has been further disturbed by the disuse of churchyards, and that legislation has imposed upon burial boards the duty, and has allowed private capital the power, of providing burial-grounds, the cost of which is to be met by special fees, do not alter the fact that burial or other mode of disposing of the dead is an absolute necessity imposed upon every individual, nor the principle that the right to burial is a common-law right, and that consequently fees paid for this right are a form of special taxation based upon the principle of benefit.

In contrast to the case of burial is that of locomotion. Good systems of traffic are absolutely necessary for the well-being of the State and of the locality. In most of the continental countries railways are administered by the State; in others, as in our own country, they are subject to certain control by the State in the interests of the public. Putting the question of railways on one side, as in no sense appertaining to local government, there are other systems of locomotion which do appertain to local government. Light railways may be constructed by county councils; tramways, as is well known, are, or can be by statute, in the hands of the municipality; hackney carriages are licensed, and to some extent controlled, by the municipality. Thus the services of locomotion have, by these provisions of the statute law, been pronounced to be either State or municipal services—services so important that in no case is it conceivable that they could be allowed to fall into decadence, or even to be restricted by the limited requirements of private capital. But important as the service of locomotion is, it is not absolutely necessary to every inhabitant. It is entirely at the option of every inhabitant whether he travels or not, although it is absolutely necessary that he should have the means of travelling if he wishes to do so, or if, for business purposes, he must do so. In crowded towns the necessity for locomotive services for workmen has a close connection with the health of the community at large. Therefore the conditions of locomotion supply two elements for consideration—namely, that the service is a necessary one to be provided, that the charge imposed to meet the cost is not compulsory upon all the inhabitants alike, but only upon those who avail themselves of it. But locomotive services in the hands of State or local authorities are either paid for, and only just paid for, entirely out of the payments made by passengers, or else, as in the case of the Irish railways, are not entirely paid for, or again, as in the case of English municipal tramways, are more than paid for out of the payments made by passengers. In the first case the taxation is according to benefit; in the second case taxation is partly according to benefit and partly according to equal rating; in the third case the passengers are taxed primarily according to benefit, and, further, an indirect tax according to consumption.

But then, it will be asked, what of the locomotive services in the hands of private owners? The same principle exactly applies as in the cases just examined. Private capital will not stand a constant loss, so the service is discontinued if loss is the result of its working. If the service just returns a small interest, equal to the interest paid for municipal capital, there is simply taxation according to benefit. But if the service returns a large dividend, we have a case of indirect taxation upon the consumer being granted for the use of private owners.

Closely connected with the service of locomotion is that of intercommunication. It is well known that the postal service and the telegraph service is in the hands of the State; but in the case of the telephone service a remarkable state of things has been allowed to develop. The trunk lines have been taken over by the State, while the local services have been left in the hands of a monopolist company, without even the benefit to be derived from competition.

The next service belonging to this group is the supply of artificial light. The necessity for this service in the general interests of the community may be shortly stated to rest upon the facts that it is required universally for domestic use and for trade purposes, and that it is supplementary to police services in the protection of property and life, by the lighting of highways and thoroughfares. In this case it is noticeable that while the gas legislation which took place in the early part of the century, before attention had been paid to any of the requirements of local government, made no provision for the rights of local authorities to acquire gas undertakings, electric-light legislation, which has only recently begun, makes due provision, not only for the acquisition of electric-light undertakings, but for the inception by local authorities of this service. The cost of this service for household purposes is met by a charge according to consumption—that is, taxation according to benefit. When this service is in the hands of private owners, in proportion as the charge is more than sufficient to pay the current municipal rate of interest, it is allowed to become remunerative to private capital by a system of indirect taxation of the consumers.

Fire insurance is a service which has a peculiar history, and of which it is worth while giving a few particulars. A law of the court of Flanders, promulgated in 1240, required damage by fire to be instantly made good by the whole locality in which it occurred. A chamber of insurance is said to have been opened at Bruges in 1310. In 1609 a proposal was made to the Count of Oldenberg that all proprietors of land should insure the houses of their tenants against fire on their paying so much per cent. annually. After the Great Fire of London the Corporation of the City were looked upon as the proper authorities to organize and conduct fire insurance. They had been asked in 1660 by Charles II. to aid in launching a plan framed by "several persons of quality and eminent citizens," but had replied that such an enterprise should be conducted by the municipality. In 1681 they appointed a committee, which suggested that fire insurance should be undertaken in the Chamber of London; and upon being instructed to prepare a plan the committee did so, and were of opinion that it would not only be of benefit to citizen insurers, but would " also be certain to raise a good revenue to the Chamber." At a subsequent meeting of the Common Council in 1681, they agreed to undertake the business, and instructed another committee to consider how a guarantee fund might be provided. Such a fund was accordingly constituted, consisting of lands and ground-rents belonging to the city, worth £100,000 at least, together with all premiums received. This civic plan caused great dissatisfaction among private projectors, who complained that the Corporation had appropriated their invention, and would reap the profits of their skill. They attacked the city in lampoons and broadsides, which are profitable reading at the present day, for they contain the arguments which capitalists now urge against local government, and they can be met by the fire insurance experience of two hundred years. The city, on November 13, 1682, determined to relinquish the undertaking, and municipal fire insurance in London collapsed, and passed into the hands of private capitalists.

In Hamburg and some other continental ports it is supposed that fire insurance was in the hands of the municipality at the time the London Corporation first took it up, and fire insurance by the State was adopted during the eighteenth century in Saxony, Silesia, Brunswick, Norway, Hanover, and Wurtemberg; later still it was adopted by, and still obtains, in the Swiss states, and it is only recently being adopted in Canada and in our Australian colonies.

In our own day several municipalities in various parts of the country are suggesting to form a scheme for insuring municipal property by their own funds.

This short account of fire insurance as a municipal

function must be supplemented by the fact that by the common law persons whose houses were burnt had ground of action against a neighbour in whose house the fire originated. This common-law right was suspended by the statute of 1707 (6 Anne, cap. 31) for three years, but was made perpetual in 1711 (10 Anne, cap. 14) and in 1774 (14 Geo. III. cap. 78). These Acts, however, did not apply to cases of culpable negligence or want of reasonable care, and to this extent, therefore, the old common-law liability still attaches. Then there is the prevention of fire. In 1707 the duty of providing means for extinguishing fires was cast upon all churchwardens of parishes within the bills of mortality, and from this has developed our present fire brigade system.

Now here we have three very important points—(1) that fire insurance was in England, and is in some foreign countries, a function of local government; (2) that liability for fire was a common-law attachment to every householder; and (3) that protection from fire is a duty imposed upon local government. Private capital could not undertake the last of these duties except at a loss, and it has, therefore, left it to local government to perform, while in respect of a portion of fire liability—namely, the liability to replace premises burnt down—it has succeeded in turning the burden into a matter of profit. But the function is a municipal function. All property within the municipal area is of concern to the municipal authority. It is the source of rating; its building is superintended by the municipal authority; its frontage line is fixed, and where possible is set back and changed for the public convenience; it is protected by the police and the fire brigade; compensation is paid for damage done by riot (see *ante*, p. 74); it benefits from all local expenditure; in fact, local government is so intimately concerned with property that fire insurance seems to be one of its elemental duties.

I will next consider the services where the system of taxation is not according to benefit. Water supply is the most important, perhaps, of these services. It conforms without qualification to all the conditions I have laid down for a function of local government. It is an elemental necessity; it is a monopoly, because of the practical impossibility of introducing any efficient system of competition; it can only be carried on by using the public thoroughfares and highways (for which no rent is charged), and by appropriating water from rivers or other water-sources belonging to the public (for which no payment is made); it is supplementary to the drainage system in its use for house sanitation; it is necessary for the public services of flushing sewers, watering roads, and extinction of fire; and the only method by which its cost can properly be met is by a system of direct taxation, not by a purchase according to consumption.

Market accommodation is of a different order to this, but has the same conditions. It is a necessary element in the due distribution of food products; it supplements the services which deal with the protection of food from adulteration and insanitary storage, and is only for public benefit. The cost of this service is met by indirect taxation in the shape of dues, tolls, and rents, which fall upon the market produce, and is paid for by the consumer. As this is a very ancient service of local government, perhaps the most ancient of all services, it is possible to trace out its development from a simple beginning to a complex system. Every village in England, especially every village founded upon the ancient organization, has its market; and every one knows what a picturesque part of English villages it is. In all the smaller places all that is required is an open space and a necessary number of hurdles to form pens for live produce. An advance upon this is the material for temporary stalls. But with the growth of the towns more is required. The markets need the sanction of laws and the organization for a daily, instead of a periodical, attendance. There is no more interesting history and no more ancient history than that of our markets, and I like to think that our own Leadenhall is on the site of the ancient Roman forum,—a site hallowed to market purposes, therefore, for at least twelve hundred years,—and that our Smithfield is on the open playground and popular market of Londoners when the qualification *field* had a real significance.

When the market service has reached the municipal stage, the expenditure is more than has been considered proper to be imposed upon direct taxation. In the village stage the expenditure is not continuous, and is only slight. In the municipal stage it is continuous, and includes the cost of building all sorts of necessary establishments for the due regulation of the market. This charge is not imposed directly upon the rates, but is met by tolls, dues, and rents paid by the merchants resorting to the market—in other words, is met by a system of indirect taxation. But, different as the taxation conditions are, the village and the municipal market are alike necessities of the community, not luxuries belonging to private commercial enterprise. The history of the establishment of the Deptford cattle-market under the jurisdiction of the City of London Corporation is the best evidence of this, and I will briefly summarize this in order to establish my point. In 1848 an Act was passed empowering the Privy Council to prohibit by order the removal of cattle from one place to another. In 1866 the power of enforcing the orders of the Privy Council within London was conferred upon the Metropolitan Board of Works, who were to appoint inspectors of diseased cattle. In 1867 an Act was passed empowering the Privy Council to regulate the landing of foreign cattle, and the Metropolitan Board were asked if they were prepared to undertake the task of establishing and maintaining a landing-place and market for foreign cattle. Nothing was done until 1869, when the Contagious Diseases Animals Act was passed, with special provisions, appointing the Corporation of the City the local authority for the whole London area, and compelling them to establish and maintain a market (*Unification of London Commission*, Mr. Kemp's evidence, ii. 384-5).

Nothing could be clearer than this short history of one Act of Parliament as proof that markets are not a luxury, but a necessity; must, therefore, be established and maintained for the public good, however the cost of them is to be met.

But, like other services of this class, the fact of the cost being met by indirect taxation has not only obscured their position among the functions properly belonging to local government, but has turned them to the private uses of individuals without any criticism that by so doing the products of taxation were being applied to private purposes.

In Saxon times we do not hear much of markets and fairs. The grant of a market, according to Kemble (*Saxons in England*, ii. 73), with power to levy tolls and exercise police authority therein, was a royalty in the period of the consolidated monarchy; but there are only two mentions of fairs in Domesday Book. This shows that the fairs which then existed were not pecuniarily valuable—in other words, were considered as public services, not private franchises. After the Norman Conquest, however, the fair was treated as a valuable franchise, derived from the prerogative of the Crown, and yielding a revenue in tolls and other profits to the king or the grantee of the franchise. The method of grant is illustrated well by the charters relating to the famous St. Giles' Fair, Winchester. The original grant by William Rufus was for three days only; five days more were added by Henry I.; six more by Stephen, and again two more by Henry II.—in all sixteen days (*Royal Commission on Markets*, i. 4).

In the case of markets, the tolls and dues had very early belonged to the king. Thus in 889 King Alfred and the sub-King of Mercia made a grant of land in London to the Bishop of Worcester, in which it was provided that "if any of his people dealt in the street or on the bank where sales took place, the king was to have his toll; but if the bargain was struck in the Bishop's *curtis*, he was to have the toll." In close connection with these rights was the system of exacting tolls in ports and harbours, and upon transport by roads, bridges, and navigable rivers, which the king might either remit in favour of individuals or might empower an individual to take, thus "in the first instance," says Mr. Kemble, "creating for them a commercial monopoly of the greatest value by enabling them to enter the market on terms of advantage." Billingsgate has been a market from the earliest times, and the *Instituta Lundoniæ*, a code of mercantile enactments of the early eleventh century, includes a minute account of the dues to be levied. Perhaps the earliest grant of a market is that of Taunton, in 904, where we get the interesting clause granting "the marketing of the said vill, which in English is called 'the town's cheaping,' and all the dues of the burgesses, etc., with all the profits incident thereto" (Kemble, *Codex Diplomaticus*, No. 1,084).

I will not trouble you with any more details on the interesting history of the market system in England, but the point to which they all converge is to show that the English system "grew up by means of royal grants of monopolies to individuals, and even when the franchise was enjoyed by a corporation its origin was independent in theory of the ordinary municipal privileges." In Scotland, however, a wholly different system prevailed. The right of market appears there as one of the ordinary privileges of a trading town, each town receiving from the Crown in very early times monopolies of buying and selling within a considerable tract of country (*Royal Commission on Markets*, i. 26).

This, then, is where the market system has been

lost sight of as an elementary function of local government, as necessary as any one of the admitted and general functions imposed by the necessities of modern times; and this is how the system of indirect taxation by the levy of tolls and rents has been allowed to be kept back from observation. The produce of market tolls and dues is now no longer a part of the king's revenue, nor of the national taxation, but for the most part it is used for keeping up the market fabric and the necessary and important duties incidental to the keeping of a market. This alteration in the object for which market tolls and dues are payable does not make them any less a system of taxation indirectly levied upon the consumers of the articles sold in the markets, and, therefore, on the double ground of being a necessary service and of being a charge upon taxation, markets are essentially a function of local government.

The next important service is that of dock accommodation and navigation. Without going into the interesting history of this subject, it suffices to say that the expenditure, whether by municipal authorities or by private companies, is met by tolls, dues, and duties levied upon the shipping frequenting the ports, except in some cases, as at Hamburg, where shipping is attracted by the port and docks being free.

Then there are the services which have not yet been undertaken at all. To what Mr. Mill has urged with regard to the importance of scientific research, whose effect cannot be ascertained or understood except after an immense amount of experimental work, accomplished at considerable cost, I would mention as a parallel the consular service of the State. No one doubts the necessity for maintaining this service, no one who reads the best of the consular reports and the valuable information they contain in the interests of commercial enterprise will say that, though the result of the expenditure on this service is not immediately apparent, it is not essential to the State. So in local government, in matters of light, of mechanical motion, of chemistry as applied to agriculture, to sewage products, to food analysis, of political economy as affecting the various questions of public taxation, citizenship, and local government, a proper provision for scientific research would benefit the community in a sense which, if it had existed even fifty years ago, it is hardly too much to say would have solved many of the difficulties which confront the statesman. If, for instance, the proper position of taxation in relation to water supply had been present to the minds of any one of the various commissions which have enquired into the London water supply, the present monopoly would not have been created or allowed to last so long

—would not, therefore, have to be bought up by the ratepayers from private capitalists. And, again, in the matter of public economics provision is required for the establishment of a regular system of prevention of waste, both for the State and for the local governments. The enormous sum lost to the nation every year by the want of a system of public economics is little thought of. In the wanton destruction of ancient and historic buildings; in the wicked waste of food products; in the duplication and absence of regulation of charitable work; in the antagonistic construction of works for different objects which might be adapted for common use; in the waste of refuse, sewage, and materials which, having served one purpose, are destroyed; in the multiplication of offices, as in the collection of taxes; in the many cases where co-ordination and combination of interests would produce a final result, while their separation and independence produce inadequate results; in the conflicts between separate interests which exist for the same purposes;—in these and other directions the establishment of a system of public economics would be an immense gain.

The functions of local government are, it will be gathered from this outline, intimately connected with the form of progress which modern civilization is finally to assume. I only wish I could have more adequately discussed this important section of our subject.

N

VI

THE DOCTRINES OF BENEFIT AND OF GENERAL UTILITY

THE general utility which is the determining qualification of the functions properly belonging to local government primarily means that every inhabitant of the locality should be directly and equally benefited by, and directly and equally concerned in, such functions. Thus health, sanitation, police, water, lighting, are self-evident examples. Secondarily, the qualification of general utility applies to services by which every inhabitant of the locality is directly benefited, but in which he may not be directly concerned. Thus locomotion, poor relief, protection of the lunatic and insane, compulsory education, housing of the working classes, land allotments to the poor, and similar functions, are examples. It may, perhaps, at first be considered that of these functions of local government some are in direct antagonism to the theory of general utility, and are sanctioned rather by the charitable and sentimental feelings of our age than by the necessity of including them among the proper subjects of local government. A closer examination of them will, I think, show that this is but a very partial interpretation of the position, and I will add it is a very mischievous interpretation.

I will select for the purpose of examination the first new function of government forced upon Tudor times—namely, the relief of the poor. Originally a matter of domestic concern of importance only to the feudal lord, to the burghal gild, to the monastery, each in their particular degree, it became a matter of general state concern when the last of these three institutions, which had principally concerned itself with the poor, had broken down by the march of events or by the direct act of the sovereign. Henry VIII. began the work of the State by attempting to legalize vagrancy (22 Hen. VIII. cap. 12). He then ordered alms to be gathered for the support of such as were unable to labour (27 Hen. VIII. cap. 25). Edward VI. next directed that houses should be provided for the poor by the devotion of good people (1 Ed. VI. cap. 3), and then that the collectors for the poor were to take down in writing what every person was "willing" to give weekly for the ensuing year, and "if any should be obstinate and refuse to give, the minister was gently to exhort him," then the bishop was to exhort him in the same manner, and if he still held out, he was to appear before the justices in sessions (5 and 6 Ed. VI. cap. 2). Next, under Elizabeth, it was prescribed if any parishioner should obstinately refuse to pay of his charity towards the relief of the poor, then the justices of the peace at quarter sessions might tax him to a reasonable weekly sum (5 Eliz. cap. 3). This led up to the famous statute (14 Eliz. cap. 5) which provided for the taxation by the justices of every parishioner, and, finally, to the still more famous statute (43 Eliz. cap. 2), which is the basis of the modern poor-law system, and which constituted the churchwardens, and four, three, or two substantial householders as overseers of the poor with power to tax every inhabitant of the parish " in such competent sum as they shall think fit."

I need go no further into details. What we have here are, first, the futile appeals to *private charity* to perform a public function, because *private duties* had hitherto performed it; secondly, the attaching of the poor-law administration to the ecclesiastical parish, because ecclesiastical institutions and property had hitherto most largely charged themselves with the administration of poor relief; thirdly, the creation of a parish authority and a parish tax, because the statesmen of Elizabeth could not see beyond the ecclesiastical aspect of poor relief.

We see in this series of legislative efforts the progress from the sentimental to the utilitarian doctrine of poor relief. Under the ecclesiastical system the principle of poor relief was never faced. Under the State system it had to be faced, because taxation had to be justified. After a hard struggle, it seems now to be admitted, both by the means adopted for actual administration and by the stated theories of expert writers, that "whenever for the purpose of government we arrive in any state of society at a class so miserable as to be in want of the common necessities of life . . . it may be expedient in a merely economical point of view to supply gratuitously the wants of even able-bodied persons, if it can be done without creating crowds of additional applicants" (Babbage, *Principles of Taxation*, p. 13). This utilitarian view of the question has been put down to the "brutal frankness" of economical investigators, but any one acquainted with the methods of meeting the difficulty of "poor relief" among the more backward societies of the world will not quarrel with the frankness of a truth which is capable of being expressed in a terminology other than that of economics (Garnier, *Annals of British Peasantry*, 33).

Let me attempt to put the argument before you, aided by such evidence as may be gained from history. Suppose a parish sufficiently populated to be able to provide work for all at wages or other reward sufficiently attractive to all, and there will be no poor.

Suppose this parish loses its power of industrial support for a portion of its inhabitants, and there will under ordinary circumstances arise a section of the people unable to live up to a moderate standard of comfort, possibly up to any standard at all. Suppose no system exists whereby this section of the people can be cared for at the minimum standard of comfort, and they will be let loose to prey upon the property and the comfort of others, to harden into an hereditary enemy to the owners of any form of property. To prevent this it will be to the interest of all owners of property to adopt some measures of relief. Now these suppositions are not merely the imaginations of a political economist, but the actual conditions of different stages of history. The village communities of early times, living chiefly on agriculture and pasture, in almost independence of each other, kept their population within the means of support afforded by the village lands by processes which do not bear examination by a world which has learnt to use the word charity. "I scarcely like to conjecture," says Mr. Garnier, in his *Annals of the British Peasantry*, "what our progenitors did with their sick and aged relatives in the heathen days of the village community. We most of us have read with a shudder of the accabatura of the Sardinians, and of the pointed axe with which the Poles despatched those of their relatives who had been robbed by nature or accident of their working or fighting energies" (p. 33). Mr. Garnier could, if he had so willed, have extended his reading into English customs as well as those of Sardinians and Poles, and he would then have found that a celebrated antiquary of the seventeenth century had seen a Wiltshire church in which a club had formerly "hung behind the church dore," so that "when the father was seaventie the sonne might fetch [it] to knock his father on the head, as effete and of no more use" (Aubrey, *Remaines of Gentilism*, 19). Plagues, famines, and scourges, like the Black Death, helped in the same direction, and no one can pretend that the doctrine of utility as interpreted by an uncivilized mind did not prevail in these times.

Was it much different at the next stage? We find our answer in the direful history of the vagrancy laws. Notwithstanding "sundrie lovabil Acts of Parliament," as it is quaintly put by Fletcher of Saltoun, Scotland in 1593 was infested by "lymmers" and "sornares," going about disguised and armed to the teeth, and compelling "gentlemen and yeomen after their daily labours to stand on their feet all night for safety of their own gear." The Golden Vale of Herefordshire in 1610, according to an Elizabethan writer, was overrun with vagrants, living on what they could steal from orchards, lands, and gardens.

In such conditions as these, existing before the

enactment of the first poor law, and, in fact, producing that enactment, we find the justification of utility as the basis of poor relief; and I have thought it necessary to indicate the existence of such evidence because it is so difficult to make people of this age look at arguments founded on abstract reasoning only. The poor law which made these ghastly facts impossible is as much a matter of utilitarian legislation as sanitation or public health, and the main effect of its benefits falls upon property. Take a parish like St. James', Westminster. By throwing off its poor, or the bulk of it, into neighbouring, or even into distant, districts, it is able to present to the owners of property a site for their buildings which is not spoiled by the loafer or the indigent, by the many unhappy surroundings which mark the presence of poverty; and the buildings so protected command higher value than they could do otherwise. This, and this alone, is the justification for calling upon the parish of St. James and other parishes similarly situated for contributions towards the poor of London generally, under a system known to London specialists as the Common Poor Fund, and it is the quantum paid by owners for protection of their property from the poor.

This being the historical evidence for the sanction of poor relief being founded on the doctrine of utility, I will now briefly touch upon the economical evidence, which is just as strong. The classification of the causes of poor relief is as follows:—

(1) Low wages paid for labour, consequent upon the competition for labour services.

(2) Misfortune and old age among those who have been dependent upon low wages.

(3) Personal disqualifications, consequent upon idleness, vice, and bad character.

The corresponding classification of the economical results of poor relief is as follows:—

(1) A grant to the employers of labour to supplement the wages they pay.

(2) A further grant to the employers of labour to supply the pension fund which they do not pay in wages; and a compassionate grant in support of the unfortunate and aged.

(3) A police charge to protect the community from the idle and the vicious, by supporting them in the poor-house or the casual ward, instead of in prison.

Now with regard to the last of these elements in the cost of poor relief, there can be no question that it is based entirely on the doctrine of utility. With regard to the first and second of these elements, it is clear that, with the exception of the compassionate grant, the granting of poor relief is in aid of wages. But, to use the words of Professor Thorold Rogers, this is a system "under which wages are supplemented, and, therefore, the prime cost of labour is diminished. The poor rate, then, is not wholly loss. It cheapens labour, and so increases rent. Take it away, and a considerable portion of that which the landowners might receive in the shape of an increased rent, due to a diminished outlay for the maintenance of the poor, would be reassumed by the farmer, in consequence of the exalted cost at which labour would be procurable" (*Journ. Stat. Soc.* xxxiii. 251).

Not only landowners and farmers are here concerned, but manufacturers and industrial undertakings. I do not, of course, affirm that it is possible to go back to the principles which governed the iniquitous statutes of labourers from 23 Edward I. to 1 James I.; but though it is useless to force economical principles into grooves they will not fit, it is necessary not to misunderstand the grooves which they carve out for themselves. In the case before us it is clear that poor relief as an element of police protection and as an element of supplemented wages is entirely a matter of general utility. There is only left the element of compassionate grant, and this must be so small in a community aided by all the resources of science such as ours that it does not afford an appreciable influence upon the total conditions for poor relief.

My assertion, therefore, that poor relief is based upon the doctrine of general utility is, I suggest, proved, and proof of this carries with it proof in respect of similar functions of local government.

At this point, it will be convenient to attempt some sort of broad definition of the functions of local government comprised in the ancient functions of county, municipality and town, and in the requirements of modern times with reference to their relationship to the doctrines of benefit and general utility. This definition I formulate as follows :—

(1) Services of general control and supervision, having for their object the securing to the public of the full benefit of competitive trading in commodities of absolute necessity or of general use.

(2) Services of administration and supply, which are of general utility to a locality, and which would not be undertaken by private enterprise unless accompanied by the right of taxation.

(3) Services of administration and supply, which are of general utility to a locality, but which are only optional in their use, and which would not be undertaken by private enterprise unless supplemented by a limited right of taxation.

(4) The power of taxation by direct tax upon assessable property, by indirect tax upon

consumers of particular commodities, or according to benefit.

I shall now have to consider these definitions of the functions of local government from another point of view altogether. We need to know in what relation the term "general utility" stands to the term "locality" in these definitions. We shall find that a new element—namely, "development"—arises out of the consideration of the relation of these two terms, and we shall have to discuss what this new element exactly means.

A service of general utility must benefit equally the whole locality concerned in it. Now the locality concerned in such a service may be a county, borough, or parish, and where this is the case there is no difficulty in determining that the county, borough, or parish, as the case may be, should be the area both of administration and taxation. This is the simple case. But a service of general utility may benefit, not the area of a county, borough, or parish, but an area differing from all these units of local government,—that is, it may benefit (1) an area outside the jurisdiction of a borough, but which is less than a county and larger than a parish ; (2) an area within the jurisdiction of a borough, but less than the area of the borough and larger than one of the constituent parts of the borough ; or (3) an area smaller than a parish. In these cases the assimilation of the area of benefit to the areas both of administration and taxation causes an apparent difficulty, and experimental legislation in attempting to deal with it has only brought about confusion. The methods adopted to meet the difficulty are two—namely, the differential taxation of a benefited area and the creation of a new area, with the result that one method has been allowed to operate in opposition to the other method in a most disastrous manner. The question is, which of these two methods accords with the principles of local government?

Let me first explain the method of differential taxation according to the area benefited. The principle of differential rating of areas according to the benefits conferred is a very old one. It is contained in the oldest sewerage Acts, in most of the improvement, lighting, and paving Acts, and is finally stamped with the authority of recent legislation in the Local Government Act of 1888. It is interesting to work this out. The statute of 6 Henry VI. cap. 5, and subsequently that of 23 Henry VIII. cap. 5, called upon all owners and others by whose default damage had happened to ditches, gutters, sewers, etc., to repair the default, and empowered the justices to distrain for the cost thereof. Under 3 and 4 Edward VI. cap. 8 special courts of commissioners were appointed to look after the sewerage of the districts allotted to their jurisdiction, and it was settled law that they were to charge an area according to the benefit conferred upon the area. This area had no relationship to parish or other local boundaries, but consisted solely of the area benefited by the expenditure. The same principle was applied to lighting, paving, and street improvements. Under old local Acts, in Shoreditch, Camberwell, and Hampstead trustees were empowered to rate all houses situated by the side of all roads lighted or within 200 yards thereof; in the case of Lambeth the limit was 500 yards, and under another Hampstead Act the limit was only 100 yards. Under the paving Acts rates were levied upon the houses situated in the roads paved or repaired, and not upon other property in the parish. Under the street improvement Acts the same principle was adopted, a good example occurring in Southwark, where the commissioners were empowered to levy a special rate upon the particular area in which the improvement was situated.

I only mention these early cases of rating of special areas according to benefits conferred to show that the principle is an early one. It was adopted in the Metropolis Management Act of 1855, where section 170 enacted that the Metropolitan Board should assess the sums for defraying their expenses, " having regard in the case of expenditure in works of drainage to the benefit derived from such expenditure by the several parts of the metropolis affected thereby." This was continued in the Act of 1858, which, for the purpose of charging expenditure upon the whole metropolis, declared that all parts of the metropolis were "deemed to be equally benefited by the expenditure under this Act." In 1862 the special area rating was repealed, but only because by that time the whole of the drainage of London was for the general benefit of the whole area. In the meantime, by section 159 of the Act of 1855, the local authorities have still the power to charge, and in some cases still do charge, a particular area of their parish or district with the cost of works which benefit that particular area only.

It is, then, by means of very easy stages that we arrive at the principle formulated in the Local Government Act, 1888, where in section 68(3) it empowers the council of any county to exempt any portion of the county from the general rating, if that portion is by law exempt, or "where the expenditure involved is by law restricted to a hundred, division, or other limited part of the county."

Differential rating is, in fact, one of the most important principles of local government to be found in early legislation. But this is not all. It is capable of almost any extension in connection with new functions which have been, or may be, imposed upon local government, and the Light Railways Act of 1896 affords a good example. From this I draw a very important conclusion, namely, that as all the requirements of assimilating the area of taxation with the area of benefit can be met by differential rating, the practice of creating new special areas for the purpose only of administering one service is no longer sanctioned by general utility, and may therefore be dismissed from consideration as an element in the principles of local government.

We are now close up to, even if we do not actually cross, a still more important principle of local government associated with the definitions we are now considering. This principle is contained in the frequent development of locality, from the parish stage to the "district" stage, from the district stage to the borough stage, and from the borough stage to the county stage, corresponding to development of local services from the parish service to the district or borough service, from the district or borough service to the county service, from the county service to the national service.

I have, then, next to deal with this new element in local government arising from the creation of new functions of government—namely, "development."

This development is twofold—a development of locality in the sense of local government and a development of services.

A development of locality is more easily understood in America than in England, but it meets us in our own country both in modern and ancient times. The growth of the municipal boroughs, of course, affords the most obvious examples. An area which at one time was a simple township, or perhaps an aggregation of townships, develops into an important industrial centre. Thus Liverpool became a borough in 1200, Hull in 1303, and Birmingham, Manchester, Bradford, and Middlesborough only since 1835.

But development of locality takes place not so obviously, but equally truly, in other connections than that of the municipal borough. Thus the development of municipal boroughs into county boroughs is an important case in point, although to some people it has not seemed anything more than a mere caprice of legislation under the Local Government Act of 1888. What has really occurred is that the locality of certain boroughs has extended beyond the original municipal areas to the suburbs beyond, and that the new locality thus formed was granted county functions as well as borough functions. In the remarkable case of London the development of the locality is even more significant. The city of London, bound within its Roman walls and a few later-formed liberties, has flowed over into the surrounding areas. At first these surrounding areas were merely knit together by their proximity to the city, and then by a system of drainage and highway administration which grouped several parishes more or less together. In 1848 the separate commissions for drainage were joined together under one commission, and the step towards consolidation was a marked one. In 1855 the loosely knit parish units were bound together under the ridiculously inaccurate title of the Metropolis, and under the ridiculously artificial machinery of the Act of 1855. This further step towards consolidation was, however, but the forerunner of the last stage, when in 1888 the locality thus formed was shaved off from the three Home Counties to form a county by itself.

Another case of development of locality is that of parishes into districts, instances of which occur all round London and near many of the great municipalities of the country; thus what was once the separated and distinct civil parishes of Barnes and Mortlake is now the Barnes district.

I hope I have made sufficiently clear what is the nature of the development of locality in the sense of local government as it is affected by new functions created from time to time, and in reference to the classification and definition of these new functions which have been attempted. My next task is to explain the development of services which takes place as a complement to, and to some extent as a cause of, the development of locality.

I will first take parish services. As the parish is an ancient local unit, it has become the sport of legislative experiments of all sorts. We have seen already how the poor law entrusted to its care fared. In other directions it was sufficiently obvious to call forth from Sir Francis Palgrave the following comment:—

"Important and multifarious duties have been improvidently accumulated upon parish officers and vestries by statute after statute. Some of these duties are very delicate, and requiring great tact and intelligence; others very odious, and affording great scope for oppression. Parliament has rendered the churchwardens and overseers officers of all work, without the slightest attention to any consistent principle or any thought about the capacity or competence of the parties to whom the duties are confided" (Palgrave, *Protest against the Municipal Commissioners' Report*, p. 20).

Let a parish be so situated as to demand the constant increase of services—to demand the application of the sanitary laws, the administration of the water supply, or any other function which does not belong to the status of parish government—and the parish without developing its locality will pass from the status of a parish to that of a district. Examples are to be found round London in plenty. Willesden, Acton, and Chiswick occur immediately to the mind.

In other examples, such as Hornsey and Tottenham, the development of services has resulted in the partition of the ancient parish into two districts.

Development of services goes on, too, in counties. Legislation has added new functions, such as technical education and light railways; natural development has in the case of London added many more services. Thus the county of London, unlike every other county in the kingdom, administers the functions of main drainage, fire brigade, and other services usually in the hands of a borough authority, while in the matter of water supply it has certain limited powers of control, and large powers of initiation for purchase and administration, in which latter function the counties of Surrey, Kent, Essex, and Middlesex obtained a footing when the matter was last before Parliament.

This is an extremely important principle of local government, and bears very directly upon the existing problems of London government. It points to the fact that whenever the area of a county grows so homogeneous in character as to demand common action in matters not ordinarily belonging to county government, because county government as a rule extends over an area which ordinarily is very far from being homogeneous in character, county government may have to detach from the municipal units within its boundaries functions which can be better administered over a larger area, and perform these functions for the larger area itself. It does something more than this. It shows that to dogmatize as to what are or should be county functions according to what has hitherto been considered such is not a safe proceeding when the principles of local government are examined into. I know it is the fashion to say that because the county authority of London administers functions which in all other places are administered by municipal authorities or district councils, that, therefore, London is in reality a borough or city, and not a county. But, on the other hand, it possesses district authorities administering many functions which ordinarily are administered by municipal authorities. On the evidence of the system of local government in London, London is certainly a county. That it may possess more powers than all other county authorities; that it may seek to regain from the municipal authority of the city some of those powers which the city obtained when it first separated itself from the county of Middlesex; that these powers should now be given back to the more fully developed county of London,—that, in short, London is what it is,—proves on the principle of development that its area has developed into a county area, and that the functions of the county council of that area have developed until, having absorbed all the common interests of the area, they combine both ordinary county functions and a few ordinary borough functions.

I should like to add a word here. The only sense in which we can properly call this great area in which we dwell and work by the proud name of "London" is that it is the county of London. People do not understand this. If in place of the county of London we have ten or any other number of independent municipal boroughs, we get a Westminster, a Paddington, a Kensington, a Poplar, and so on; perhaps we should get once more that ridiculous title, Metropolis—a Greek word, applicable to Canterbury as the mother city of ecclesiastical England; but in any case we shall lose the name of London, except for the single square mile of the ancient city. At present I confess to a singular pride in the fact that the capital of the British Empire is not a borough, not a city, but a county; and as a Londoner born, and descended from several generations of Londoners, I want to claim the right of the name of London for the true London; nay, I want more than the mere name—I want the thing itself. And if these lectures have succeeded in bringing out the principles of local government, they will at least have proved the extreme importance of fixing upon and understanding the locality before you deal with its system of government. The council of the county of London is a body whose life is limited to three years, when the county—the *communitas*—renews that life. The county of London is the thing to get definitely fixed in one's mind—the area that has grown up from parishes, and liberties, and townships, and hamlets, each with separate governments, separate interests, separate Acts of Parliament, into a great and powerful county, worthy to be the capital of the empire, and containing common interests, aspirations, and hopes.

A still further case of development is represented by the service which goes on developing until it becomes a national, instead of a local, service. An instance is to be found in prisons. On the 12th July, 1877, the Prisons Act was passed, giving legislative sanction to the development which had been taking place in the matter of prisons, from a local service to an Imperial service. " On and after the commencement of this Act," is the reading of section 16, "the obligation of any county, riding, division, hundred, liberty, franchise, borough, town, or other place having a separate prison jurisdiction to maintain a prison or to provide prison accommodation for its prisons, shall cease"; and of section 4, "All expenses incurred in respect of the maintenance of prisons and of the prisoners therein shall be defrayed out of moneys provided by Parliament"; while section 5 provides for the transfer of the prisons and "the furniture and effects belonging thereto, . . . also all powers and jurisdiction at common law, or by Act of Parliament, or by charter," shall be transferred to, and vested in, and exercised by one of Her Majesty's Principal Secretaries of State. I will refer to one more detail of this statute. Section 6 provides that "for the purpose of aiding the Secretary of State in carrying into effect the provisions of this Act . . . Her Majesty may . . . at any time . . . by warrant under her sign manual appoint any number of persons to be commissioners during Her Majesty's pleasure."

I do not know any statute which illustrates at one and the same time so many of the points I have been endeavouring to lay before you. There are the old historical localities mentioned by name as the basis of prison jurisdiction—a list of localities which takes us back far into Anglo-Saxon times. There is the reference to the prescriptive chartered and legislative rights which these localities possessed with regard to prisons and prisoners. There is the transfer to the State of all jurisdiction and all rights, and there is the appointment by the State of a body of commissioners to carry on the functions of a service which had developed from a local to an Imperial service.

It is obvious that police comes closely up to the case of prisons. The ancient system of police is now entirely obsolete, and the county police system is practically the rule. Boroughs may, and do, have their own special police forces, but it has been the policy of the Police Acts to encourage a consolidation of county and borough police. In the case of London and the Home Counties, consolidation has taken a special shape, as usual with London. The Metropolitan Police is under a Commissioner appointed by the Home Office, and is really a government force controlled by the Home Office. All these separate forces, with their tendency to consolidation, are under Government inspection and Government subsidy. Up to 1875 the Government paid one-fourth of the pay and clothing; then this was increased to one-half; while in 1891 a special grant was made by Government to the pension fund. In Scotland the same principle obtains as in England, but in Ireland the force is entirely a Government force.

Alike, then, in administration and in fiscal matters the Government has an important share in police administration. In the case of the Metropolitan Police that share is more than ordinary. It has constituted the force a national, as well as local, police. The Imperial dockyards at Sheerness are policed by the London force. When Surrey requires more police to protect persons and property during the Epsom races, men are sent down from London; when the Czar of all the Russias, or any other potentate, visits our own sovereign, London police attend him at Balmoral, at Portsmouth, or wherever the Court functions extend; when a great criminal like Jabez Balfour escapes to South America, the London police are used to fetch him back; when dynamitards or other national criminals are arrested, the London police are employed — the London criminal investigation department is a national institution, not a London one. In the interests of the local taxpayer this tendency towards, or rather this partial, nationalization of the police force should be recognised and grappled with. At present it is neither one thing nor the other. We in London, for instance, do not know whether we are paying for our own local force or for a national force; but I suggest that the whole tendency of police administration points to central government, rather than local.

Nowhere is the principle of development better exemplified than in the poor-law system. We have seen the fatuous struggle that ushered in the early statutory laws upon this subject, the struggle which was caused by a refusal to recognise that poor relief had grown beyond the stage of private or ecclesiastical charity. I have now to show that this recognition, tardily accepted by philosophical and economical writers, has never been translated into legal recognition.

The parish unit struggled for some time with the

burden cast upon it by Elizabeth's poor law; with what success is known to those who have studied the disastrous, if not disgraceful, events which forced on the great poor-law reform of 1834, with what result may be judged by the fact that seven millions of public money was spent in one year upon poor relief among a total population of about eleven millions, and was administered "by more than 2,000 justices, 15,000 sets of overseers, and 15,000 vestries, acting always independently of each other and very commonly in opposition" (Fowle, *Hist. Poor Law*, p. 74).

But the reform of 1834, great as it was, leaves chaos still the prevailing feature. Amalgamation of parishes into unions for administrative and taxation purposes was accompanied by central supervision by a State department. This in turn has been followed by central taxation—that is, the allocation of Imperial taxes to poor-law purposes. So that we have 648 local administrative bodies and 1 central body, 648 different rates to meet the charges for poor relief and Imperial taxation doled out upon a plan which has the effect of introducing the county area and the county authorities into the elements which finally determine the incidence of poor-law taxation. This is not all. The poor-law system, though it extends through the whole area of the country, and though it is based upon the parish unit, has disregarded every local government area. Of the 62 administrative counties there is not one, not even London, which contains an undivided number of poor-law areas; of the 64 county boroughs there are only six which wholly contain an undivided number of poor-law areas; and of the 239 municipal boroughs very few, indeed, are conterminous with poor-law areas. These facts reveal the poor-law system as a network of authorities having, indeed, the qualification of representation, but not the necessary qualification of locality. The poor-law system, I would go so far as to say, is not a part of local government at all. For administrative purposes, it is more intimately associated with the central department than with localities, and it is becoming, and will, if I mistake not, more and more become, a national function, rather than a local.

If the history of the law of removal and settlement—a vital part of the poor-law system, though now mitigated from the extreme form in which it appeared in the law of Charles II.—tells us anything, it tells for the nationalization of the poor law. In 1851 Mr. George Coode made a report to the Poor-Law Board in which he strongly advocated the entire abolition of this hateful law, and the opening paragraph of his report places the question very succinctly before us. "The law," he says, "is now of too ancient a date and too universal an operation to allow a single case to exist through which we might discover the manner in which a labouring man would avail himself of the common resources of his country if he were free from these laws, or how a parish would act in their absence, or what would be the effect of freedom of movement on wages, or what would be the facilities for movement and habitation of the labouring class, or their command of comfort for themselves and families, or the connected effects on the employers of labour, and the progress of the industrial arts, and the application of capital, or on pauperism, or vagrancy, or taxation. All these matters have been affected and their character determined by the operation for nearly two hundred years of the most stringent, despotic, and searching law that ever controlled the domestic condition and industrial habits of a nation. . . . The hardships of removal to poor people, the apprehensions of the inert and pauperized labourers of the strange and hostile parish, the successful or unsuccessful speculations of employers in their deteriorated industry, the success or failure of parish policy in the use of this law and in evading their responsibilities for the necessities it creates, may be abundantly illustrated by every day's experience; but all such illustrations are nothing in the matter while we are unable to compare them with the condition and relations of a free English labourer having the right and born and bred to it of carrying his person and using his faculties wherever his own judgment might lead him. Without the example of a free labourer for a standard, it is manifestly impossible to estimate the effect of this legal bondage on those subjected to it or corrupted by it."

This is striking and remarkable language, and, justified as it was in 1851, I question whether it is not as applicable now, even though the terms of the law of settlement have been made lighter and the area wider. The restrictive forces of such a law cannot, as Mr. Coode says, be measured, but they at least point to the only remedy—namely, abolition. But their abolition means making the relief of the poor a national, not a local, service. Already it is financially dependent to a very large extent upon national taxation and national superintendence and inspection. Indeed, it is not going too far to say that no Government would dare again to leave the administration of the poor law to the unfettered discretion and power of local authorities. Of course, I do not suggest that in the hands of the State the system now pursued could or should be continued—a theory which is always present when this subject is being discussed by those who oppose nationalization. But for my present purpose it is not necessary to discuss methods by which nationalization could be brought about; all that I am anxious to do is to point out two very important factors which show the tendency in that direction—namely, (1) the relaxation in the law of settlement and the beneficial economical effect upon the labouring poor by its total abolition, and (2) the large proportion of cost which is met by national, and not local, taxation, and the accompanying increase of control by the State over the local administration.

I have one more point to establish from the doctrines of benefit and general utility, and this is a very important one. Functions which are performed because they are of general utility enure to the benefit of those who can command the means of best placing these services at the disposal of the community, and these are the owners of property. To have the advantage of local government services a person must live in a house which places those services within reach, and competition for such a house secures to the owner the benefit of all services performed for the locality. This is an important principle, and enters largely into the question of taxation, by which services of local government are met.

There is no need, I am sure, to emphasize the importance of these doctrines of benefit and general utility. They operate in developing the functions and localities of local government; they explain the process by which functions become national instead of local, county instead of borough, borough instead of parish; they show the natural elasticity of local government; and they fix upon property as the right medium through which to provide the necessary taxation.

VII

THE ELEMENT OF LOCAL TAXATION

WHEN I look back upon the dry technicalities which it has been my lot to bring before you, I confess I am somewhat staggered by the incompleteness of the results attained. I cannot hide from myself that here and there further illustration is needed, that almost everywhere the terminology of our subject is extremely incomplete, and oftentimes inconsistent, and that the vastness of the field to be covered prevents the mind from readily taking in all that is demanded of it. And when I come to my final task, the deficiencies of my work appear to be multiplied.

Having discussed the two elements of "general utility" and "locality" with reference to the functions of local government, I have now very shortly to consider, in connection with the definitions of these functions which I gave in a previous lecture, the relationship of taxation—the ultimate sanction of local, as of State, government to the general principles which have been examined. You will remember that these functions formed two classes, one consisting of services which have never been allowed to become remunerative to private capital, the other of services which have been allowed to become remunerative to private capital; and we ascertained that the taxation involved by these services, whether in the hands of local authorities or of private enterprise, was of three kinds—(1) taxation according to benefit, (2) taxation of consumers, (3) taxation according to equal rating.

The present system of Imperial and local taxation is a dual system. The total of both is the measure of the impost upon each class of taxpayer and each interest paying taxes, but there is no existing means of knowing this total. No county, borough, or town authority can ascertain this total, or ever claims a right to do so; no Government department attempts to ascertain this total or any equivalent of it, and does not even formulate its taxation statistics sufficiently correctly for any student to obtain the information for himself. And thus legislation is effected in the dark. The sweeping changes made during the last eight years by the Local Government Act of 1888, the Finance Act of 1894, and the Agricultural Rates Act of 1896, have been accomplished without regard to the interlacing of Imperial with local taxation and the result produced by the changes. In Imperial taxation the changes tend for simplicity and equity; in local taxation they have produced something like chaos; and in the case of the

Agricultural Rates Act economical injustice. In the meantime, the Commission on Financial Relations between Great Britain and Ireland have reported in favour of the principle that Imperial taxation should be assessed upon the units first, before the assessment is made to fall upon the individual taxpayer. An extension of this principle to the localities would practically take us back to the system of the fifteenth century, and I am not at all sure that the demand is not an outcome of the present absolute indifference and ignorance as to the incidence of the combined Imperial and local taxation when it finally reaches the individual who pays. If every county authority had concerned itself for a series of years with the incidence of taxation upon the taxpayers within its jurisdiction, and had sought through the machinery of the Exchequer grants to get admitted injustice remedied, we should not have had the Agricultural Rates Act, with its system of uniform application to totally different conditions, and we should not have had the absurdly artificial method of apportioning Exchequer grants under the provisions of the Act of 1888.

Now the first principle of taxation is that the taxpayer shares with all other taxpayers of the same class as himself a fair and equal—to use the adjectives of legislation—charge, tax, or rate. For the purposes of Imperial taxation each taxpayer shares with the taxpayers of the United Kingdom two of the direct taxes—estate duty, income tax—and the indirect taxes—general stamps, customs and excise duties and licenses, postal and telegraph stamps; he shares with the taxpayers of Great Britain only the inhabited house duty; but he shares with the counties of Great Britain the land tax. Thus there are three gradations of sharing in Imperial taxation.

In the case of local taxation the gradations and complexities of sharing are much greater. Thus each taxpayer may share with the taxpayers of a larger area than the county or borough, as, for instance, in the case of Greater London, as it is called, for the purpose of police, Bootle and Liverpool combined, for the purposes of water, and other instances. Beyond this special area for sharing taxation every taxpayer shares with all other taxpayers of the county or county borough, then with the taxpayers either of the borough or district, then with the taxpayers of the union, and finally with the taxpayers of the parish.

On the face of it, therefore, the system of local taxation, as compared with Imperial taxation, is a complex subject; but if I were to attempt to describe all its peculiarities, all the differentiations, and all the changes of incidence, I should not be able to deal with the subject as part of these lectures. Fortunately for my present purpose, this is not a necessary task. I am not so much concerned with the general principles of taxation as I am with ascertaining what the main principle of taxation is so far as it affects the subjects I am now concerned with.

In a previous lecture, you will remember, I led you through the somewhat dry details which help to determine the element of taxation in connection with services which are still partly withheld from local government. I pointed out that the charge imposed for burials, locomotion, gas and electric light, and similar services, was taxation according to benefit, instead of equal sharing. It is, therefore, extremely important to know that according to the views of those who originated the system of local taxation, and according to the views of those who first paid the demands of local taxation, taxation went according to benefit. So clear were our ancestors on this point that when taxation by co-sharing was adopted they applied to it the principle of taxation by benefit by confining taxation to areas, limited, not by the jurisdiction of a local authority, but by the extent of the benefit conferred. From this I have already adduced very important conclusions with reference to the jurisdiction of the governing authority, and I now have to show how it occurs in taxation.

Let us look at the oldest rates imposed by positive law. I cannot say the oldest rates absolutely, because these are the county, hundred, township, and tithing rates, all of common-law origin, and assessed upon individuals in a manner not now easily discoverable. But of the oldest rates imposed by positive law we first have the poor rate. By the 43rd of Elizabeth this was imposed expressly upon lands, houses, tithes impropriate, propriations of tithes, coal mines, and saleable underwoods. Thus, say the Commissioners on Local Taxation, in 1843, notwithstanding that defined persons are liable in respect of these properties, it will be found upon examination that the poor's rate is in its operation a property tax, and not a personal tax (p. 18). The judges followed this principle, for in determining how "inhabitants, and parsons, and vicars"—also mentioned in the statute as persons to be taxed—were to be taxed, they were guided by the principle that by implication the property liable to be taxed belonging to these three classes of persons, although not identical, should be analogous with the property liable expressly, and the Courts also held that the property to be liable by implication should be local, and visible, and productive of profit. Principles which applied to the early poor rate applied to all the local taxes. To some of them because they were expressly levied as a part of the poor rate; to others with additional force, inasmuch as the statutes under which they were imposed did not even refer to the persons liable, but only to the property upon which the tax was to be levied. This is especially the case with the old highway rate and the lighting and watching rate. Again, the expressions to be found relating to the church rate referred to the property, and rarely to the persons; and the sewers rate was directed to be imposed upon lands, tenements, and rents (*Report of Commissioners*, 1843, pp. 18–25).

These indications of the object of the legislature in imposing the early taxes upon property are confirmed by later proceedings. The Act of 59 Geo. III. cap. 12 enabled the inhabitants of a parish, assembled in vestry, to direct that owners might be rated personally, instead of occupiers, for properties under £20 per annum and more than £6, and another instance of substituted liability to pay is in the case of the rate for building a county lunatic asylum, for which it was provided that the justices at quarter sessions may, if they unanimously agree, direct every tenant at rackrent to deduct one-half of the rate from the rent he pays (*Commissioners' Report*, 1843, p. 38). I am not, of course, concerned with the absurdity of the provisos to these two Acts, but I direct attention only to their principle.

In the first place I have to remark that the legislators who imposed the first local tax were in a far better position than ourselves to estimate the result of local taxation. They were applying it to virgin soil. They saw the conditions which existed without taxation, and they had to apprise the conditions which would result from taxation. They also had to convince the payer of these new imposts that they had good grounds for their new departure. Can we believe, then, that they were wrong in asserting that taxation should go according to benefits? and, consequently, that as it was imposed upon property it benefited property? They, looking forward to the economical probabilities of the imposition of taxation, and we, looking backward upon the ascertained results of taxation, ought to meet somewhere on common ground. I think that common ground will be found in the doctrine that the expenditure which produces local taxation is a benefit to property.

This brings me to an important phase of the subject, often occurring in official documents, and often referred to in discussions in Parliament and elsewhere. Thus in a very able report upon the local taxation of Scotland, issued in 1896, we have a definite attempt to define and apportion local taxation into (1) remunerative and (2) non-remunerative taxation. We have met with the first term before in these lectures—namely, when I was discussing the conflict between private capital and local government, and where it was used in so limited and erroneous a fashion. Let me hasten to observe that its reintroduction here has nothing whatever to do with its dismissal in a former lecture; in other words, I shall in reviving the term have nothing to do with the way in which the term has been misused.

All that has been adduced in previous lectures as to the origin of local government, as to the methods of determining the functions of local government, and as to the principles which govern taxation as a means of meeting the expenditure incurred by local government, will prepare you for the proposition that the services rendered through the machinery of taxation are as real as the services rendered through any other means. It was found difficult, if not impossible, to separate the functions of local government from the enterprise of private industry by any difference in character, and all that was finally accomplished was to separate these two classes of undertakings by the difference in the manner in which best results to the consumer were to be obtained. In the case of private enterprise economical competition brought about the best results; in the case of functions undertaken by local government there is no competition to produce the best results, but the machinery of government supplied them. When, therefore, we come finally to consider what local taxation is, we are more prepared for the qualification remunerative than for the converse.

This is worth a little further consideration. The preparation of land for municipal work was originally provided for by private estate Acts, and it will not surprise you that the line of development from private to municipal service is traceable from the Statute Book.

Thus the first stage is represented by those Acts where all works are imposed upon the owners as a direct charge. An example of this occurs in the Brownswood Estate Act of 1821 (1 and 2 Geo. IV. cap. 44), one of the Prebendary estates of St. Paul's Cathedral, in the parish of Hornsey, Middlesex. The sixth section of this Act puts it upon the lessees "to lay out and appropriate any part or parts of the said premises as or for roads, ways, or passages for the use and convenience of the tenants and occupiers thereof, or as or for public streets, squares, roads, paths, or passages, and to make drains, sewers, or other easements" in return for "the best and most improved yearly rent or rents that can be had or gotten for the same." The next stage is when the lessees are formed into a commission with regularly constituted rating powers. An example of this occurs in the Southampton Estate Act of 1801 (41 Geo. III. cap. 131). Although earlier in point of date, this Act is later in point of development, and is the model for a whole series of Acts which still govern certain parts of St. Pancras. By it "the owner, or owners, of the freehold and inheritance, his, her, and their heirs and assigns," together with certain persons named in the Act (the lessees), are "appointed commissioners for carrying this Act into execution," and it is imposed upon the commissioners "to cause the several streets, squares, and other public passages and places to be made and set out within the limits of this Act to be paved"; also "to be cleansed, lighted, watched, and watered" (sect. 13); "to cause such lamp-irons and lamp-posts to be put up or fixed upon or against the walls or pallisadoes of any of the houses, tenements, or buildings and inclosures, or in such other manner within the said intended streets, squares, or other public passages and places as they shall think proper"; "to cause to be painted, engraved, or described . . . the name by which each respective street, square, lane, etc., is to be properly called or known"; "to cause all or any of the streets, squares, etc., to be watered," for which purpose they may "cause such number of wells and pumps to be dug, sunk, and made as they shall think necessary" (sect. 18); and, finally, "to appoint such number of watchmen and patroles" as they shall think proper, providing "them with proper arms, ammunition, weapons, and cloathing for the discharge of their duty." In return for these services the commissioners are empowered to levy "one or more rate or rates, assessment or assessments, . . . upon all houses, shops, warehouses, coach-houses, stables, cellars, vaults, buildings, and tenements in any of the said streets, squares, etc." (sect. 37).

I think these are remarkable provisions. In the first case we have the owners carrying out works and services, which are now works and services of local government, at their own cost and in return for what rent they could obtain; in the second case we have owners formed into a body of commissioners for carrying out a greatly extended list of works and services, including the remarkable provisions as to armed watchmen and patrols, which are now works and services of local government, in return for a rateable charge upon property. In both cases the charge or cost of the services is made according to the principle of benefit. In the first case it is according to the principle of benefit pure and simple; in the second case it is according to the principle of benefit so far as the area of charge is concerned, and according to the principle of co-sharing so far as each property within the area of charge is concerned. This system of co-sharing has been extended until it is looked upon as the sole "principle" of local taxation—the co-sharing of a burden, not the co-sharing of a benefit. In restoring the factor of "benefit" to the principles of local government, much more is gained than I can possibly sketch out to you now. I first applied to the services administered, and proper to be administered, by local government, and I pointed out that these services were not burdens, but benefits, and that private capital had first introduced a wrong terminology and then worked upon this error to its own aggrandizement. I have now applied to taxation which is the ultimate sanction of local government, and I point out that the principle of benefit is equally well proved. The system of co-sharing, used so largely as working machinery, may or may not be equitable in all cases, may or may not be wise in all cases. It is admittedly equitable and wise in the case of water-rating, because water is a necessity of health and sanitation, and the results of keeping the very poor in good sanitary condition accrues to the benefit of the rich; though some people cannot yet distinguish this function of water supply from that of any other commodity to be bought like a bottle of champagne. On the other hand, the principle of co-sharing would not be wise and would not be equitable in the case of gas-rating; and so here the principle of taxation according to benefit is maintained. There are some who argue that locomotion should be administered on the principle of taxation according to co-sharing, instead of taxation according to benefit. So long as all arguments are conducted with open eyes as to facts and as to results, so long as principles are kept to the front, we may hope that decisions will be true.

This is as far as I can now go into the question of taxation as it relates to the principles of local government which have been the subject-matter of these lectures. I am not at all sure that what I have said is enough to make the points clear, and I am quite sure that it is not enough to make the whole subject clear. It is a subject by itself; but is so intimately connected with the substance of local government that it could not be passed over in silence. All that I have wished to do is to establish the principle that local taxation is a payment for benefits conferred. When the taxpayer pays in return for benefit, as for a burial fee, for gas supply, the burden is in exact proportion to the benefit conferred. When the taxpayer pays in proportion to commodities consumed, as for market produce, for shipping dues, etc., the burden is only partly in proportion to benefit conferred. When the taxpayer pays in proportion to the rent of property, the burden is sometimes greater and sometimes less than the benefit conferred, the justification for the inequality being that the poorer parts of the community must not be allowed to fall behind the richer parts in securing and utilizing the benefits. Thus in each class of taxation benefit is the governing principle. The aggregation of all the benefits tends to accrue, if it does not actually accrue in all cases, into the hands of owners of property, because it is by means of property that the taxpayers can alone obtain the benefits conferred by the services of local government.

VIII

CONCLUDING DEFINITIONS

I HAVE now finished these lectures, and if I may sum them up in a series of brief definitions, I would say—

(1) That a locality is formed by the common interests of the community.

(2) That all the inhabitants of the locality—Londoners, Yorkshiremen, Liverpuldians and the rest—are the community of the locality.

(3) That locality, formed in the manner stated, is the foundation of local government.

(4) That the elected council is the responsible executive body, acting on behalf of, and not in substitution of, the *communitas*.

(5) That the benefit of the *communitas* is the object and result of local government.

(6) That the services administered, and proper to be administered, are services of general utility.

(7) That the value of the services enures primarily to the owners of property.

(8) That the cost of services is met by taxation which represents the amount of benefit conferred, not the amount of burden imposed.

(9) That the burden of taxation only arises when the amount paid as taxation is in excess of the amount of benefit conferred; the burden of taxation being the excess payment, not the total amount paid.

These definitions can, of course, only be considered as preliminary conclusions obtained from a first survey of the subject. I hope they will be accepted as logically proceeding from the investigation which has been attempted in these lectures. They are in no sense final. Further investigation will take place, and will both modify these definitions and produce further definitions. But the value of even preliminary definitions is that they serve as a convenient halting-place from which to proceed further. I have endeavoured in this first course of lectures to present a wide survey of the subject rather than a detailed analysis; to indicate its scope and interest rather than to exhaust any one of its phases; to establish how absolutely essential it is, in the interest of public thought, that the principles of local government should be defined and generally understood rather than to attempt the huge task of definition within the compass of a single term.

NOTES AND ILLUSTRATIONS

LECTURE I

1. The electorate (pp. 2, 3) is not at all an easy subject to define. There are a great many Acts of Parliament which deal with it, and there are many anomalies. The differences between the electorate for local government and the electorate for the imperial government are not very many, though they are important in principle. Perhaps the analysis on the next page of the London electorate will assist the reader to understand the point advanced in the text.

In all cases the right to vote is confined to British subjects, and there are certain disqualifications, such as misdemeanours, corrupt practices, receipt of poor relief, etc.

2. The Municipal Corporations Act, 1835 (5 & 6 Wm. IV. c. 76) is a very important factor in the history of Local Government in England. Section 1 (quoted on p. 4) follows the recital that at sundry times divers bodies corporate had been constituted within the cities, towns, and boroughs of England and Wales, to the intent that the same might for ever be and remain well and quietly governed; and that it was expedient that the Charters by which the said bodies corporate were constituted should be altered in the manner thereinafter appearing. The effect of this enactment was not only to sweep away all usages, customs, charters, grants, and local and other Acts of Parliament, which were contrary to, or even inconsistent with, the other provisions of the Act, but also to confirm them in all other respects (*see* Grant on Corporations, p. 342). Section 6 provides that after the first election of councillors under the Act, the body corporate of each borough shall take and bear the name of the Mayor, Aldermen, and Burgesses of such borough. The effect of this section was to change the style of the corporation of the greater number of the boroughs and cities scheduled to the Act. But notwithstanding this change of name, and notwithstand-

Class of Elector.	Qualification.	County Electors.	Parochial Electors.	Parliamentary Borough Electors.	Parliamentary County Electors.
1. Adult males not being peers, service occupiers, or constables [this disqualification of constables does not apply to the Metropolitan or City police]	£10 occupation Or household	486,340	486,340	486,340	—
2. Joint occupiers of premises being in the joint occupation of several persons as owners or tenants	£10 occupation				
3. Service occupiers	Household	—	20,623	20,623	—
4. Lodgers	£10 unfurnished lodgings	—	59,630	59,630	—
5. Women who occupy qualifying property	£10 occupation or household				
6. Peers who occupy qualifying property		96,198	96,198	—	—
7. Joint occupiers of property not included under heading 2	£10 occupation				
8. Owners	Ownership of property, whether of freehold, leasehold or copyhold tenure				
9. Married women	Ownership of property (as in No. 8) or £10 occupation or household in respect of property for which the husband does not qualify	—	10,837	—	—
10. Liverymen of the City of London	Freemen of the City who are also liverymen of one of the livery companies	—	—	7,498	—
11. Freeholders of at least forty shillings; freeholders for life or lives of an annual value above forty shillings and below five pounds (if the property is occupied by the owner, or was acquired before 1832, or was acquired by marriage, marriage settlement, descent, devise, or accession to office); freeholders, copyholders, or holders by any other tenure for life or lives of an annual value of at least five pounds; leaseholders where the leasehold was originally created for a term not less than 60 years, and of a yearly value of at least five pounds; leaseholders where the leasehold was originally created for a term of not less than 20 years, and of a yearly value of at least fifty pounds.	See col 1.	—	—	—	13,246
		582,538	673,628	574,091	13,246

ing the radical alteration of the constitution of most of the Corporations by the repeal contained in Section 1, and the substantive provisions of the Act, it is settled law that "the effect of the statute was not to create a new Corporation in any case, but merely to continue the old Corporation, so that all the rights, claims, franchises, privileges, prescriptions, and customs, as well as all the debts, liabilities, and duties of the Corporation as it stood on the day the statute passed, remain and inhere in the remodelled Corporation, so far as they are not contrary to, or inconsistent with, the provisions of the Act" (*see* Grant on Corporations, p. 343, and the cases there cited).

3. The principal schemes for the government of London (p. 11) put forward for legislation are sufficiently diverse, and many of them are opposed to all principles of local government, but the private schemes never advanced to the dignity of consideration of Parliament are still worse in this respect.

The principal private scheme is that favoured by the City of London Corporation of a series of ten independent municipal boroughs centred round the City of London. This would confine the name of London to the City area only. The Parliamentary schemes include recommendations of Royal Commissions in 1837 and 1854, and of Select Committees of the House of Commons in 1861, 1866 and 1867. The Bills introduced into the House of Commons for the reform of London are as follows :—

Government Bill of 1856. In April, 1856, Sir George Grey introduced a Bill founded upon the recommendations of the Commissioners of 1854. By its provisions the City was re-divided into sixteen wards, of more equal area than those then existing. Each ward was to be represented by one Alderman and five Common Councillors. Aldermen were to be appointed for six years, one-half of their number going out every three years. The Lord Mayor was to be elected by the Common Council, and all persons qualified to be Common Councillors were eligible for this office. The same qualification was adopted for the Sheriffs. The City Auditors were to be elected from the same class of people not being members of the Common Council. The Court of Aldermen was abolished, and the election of all the principal City officers was vested in the Common Council, with the exception of the Recorder, who was to be elected by the Aldermen. The custom of the admission of brokers was abolished, and the market jurisdiction of the City was taken away; also the exclusive rights of trading, metage dues, street tolls, and the exclusive rights of fellowship porters. The Court of Hustings, the Court of St. Martin's-le-Grand, and some other old City courts, were abolished, and the Recorder was in future to be the Judge of the Lord Mayor's Court. Aldermen were placed on the same footing as justices of a county, and the City was brought within the Metropolitan Police Court District. The provisions of the Municipal Corporation Act as to the charging or alienation of property were applied to the City. On the 20th of June the Government announced that there was no reasonable prospect of being able to pass the Bill during the Session, and it was therefore withdrawn with the expressed intention of re-introducing it in the following Session. This, however, was not done.

Government Bill of 1858. This was the Bill of 1856, modified in certain respects. By its provisions the Common Council was increased from 96 to 112 by allowing each of the sixteen proposed wards to send six Councillors and one Alderman to the Common Council. The Aldermen were to hold office for life, but the power of removal upon representations from the wards was vested in the Common Council. The Bill was read a second time on February 12th, after which it was referred to a select Committee. Eventually the Committee reported, and then the City petitioned the House of Commons that the Bill should be referred back to the Select Committee, and that the City should be heard by Counsel against the Bill. The Government resisted this, but the delay occasioned was so great that the Bill had to be withdrawn.

Government Bill of 1859. In 1859 Sir George Cornewall Lewis introduced a Bill founded upon that of Sir George Grey of 1858. The Bill was introduced too late, and had to be withdrawn, but on the 30th of January, 1860, Sir George Lewis re-introduced the Bill. In its new form, the measure dealt only with a few changes in the City constitution. It was withdrawn on the 30th of July.

Mr. Mill's Bills of 1867. In 1867 Mr. Mill introduced a Bill for the purpose of establishing separate Municipal Corporations in the several districts of the Metropolis, and also a Bill for the establishment of a central Municipal Government. The first measure provided for the division of the metropolis into ten boroughs, besides the City. Each borough was constituted a body corporate with Mayor, Aldermen, and Burgesses. The provisions of the Municipal

Corporation Act were applied to each borough so created. The second Bill, which was introduced later in the Session, was for the establishment of a central Municipal Government. The Bills were re-introduced by Mr. Mill in practically the same form in 1868; but the Bill dealing with the constitution of a central Corporation was stopped in consequence of due notice of its introduction not having been advertised for the benefit of the City in the preceding November.

Mr. Buxton's Bills of 1869. These Bills were practically the same as those introduced by Mr. Mill in 1868, and were introduced by Mr. Buxton, as Mr. Mill was no longer in Parliament. The Home Secretary assured the House that the subject would receive the attentive consideration of the Government, and Mr. Buxton withdrew the Bills.

Mr. Buxton's Bills of 1870. As the Government did not act upon their assurance and introduce any measure in the ensuing Session, Mr. Buxton, in 1870, introduced three Bills dealing with the government of London. They were intituled respectively: "The Municipal Boroughs Bill," "The Corporation of London Bill," and "The County of London Bill." The Municipal Boroughs Bill divided London into nine boroughs, besides the City. The vestries were abolished, but the former proposals of separate Mayors and Aldermen did not re-appear in this measure. They were replaced by Wardens, one in each borough. The number of Councillors varied, and the boroughs thus constituted were placed under the provisions of the Municipal Corporations Act, 1835. The Corporation of London Bill had for its object the creation of the Metropolitan Corporation of London, and the continuance of the Municipal Government of the City of London. The government of the City of London is left intact, with the exception that its chief officer is to be called Warden, and not Mayor. The Court of Aldermen is abolished, but its functions are preserved. A Central Corporation is constituted, consisting of the Lord Mayor, Aldermen, and Metropolitan Councillors. The Lord Mayor to be elected by the Metropolitan Council from among the Aldermen. The Warden of the City of London was to be the Deputy Lord Mayor. The Metropolitan Council was to consist of 167 members. The County of London Bill, introduced along with the other two, was for the purpose of constituting the Metropolitan area one county. The Bills were read a second time, and referred to a Select Committee, and were ultimately withdrawn.

Lord Elcho's Bill of 1875. This Bill was prepared by the Metropolitan Municipal Association. It embodied the provisions of previous measures, and extended the Corporation over the whole metropolitan area. It was introduced by Lord Elcho and Mr. Kay-Shuttleworth. The principle of the Bill was not the absolute creation of an original constitution; but the extension to the whole metropolis of a modified constitution of the City Corporation. The electoral body of the new Municipality was to be composed of the present City electors, and those at present qualified to vote at the election of vestrymen. The governing body was to consist of the Mayor, Aldermen, and Councillors. The Lord Mayor was to be elected by the Municipal Council; any one qualified to vote for a Councillor might be selected for the office. Three Aldermen were to be elected from each of the metropolitan districts. One-third of the Aldermen were to retire every year. The Municipal Councillors were to be elected by the present electoral body with the cumulative system of voting—five members to be elected by each ward. The powers and functions of the Municipal Council were to include all those possessed by the governing bodies of the Corporation of the City, by the Corporation of Westminster, by the Metropolitan Board of Works, by Vestries and District Boards, and by the different bodies of commissioners and trustees discharging municipal functions in various parts of the metropolis. The property and the right to tolls and duties in the hands of the various governing bodies of the metropolis were transferred to the new Municipality for the public benefit of the metropolis; but, with regard to the City, it was provided that, except by consent of its representatives, the Council should not expend the proceeds of the City property otherwise than for the benefit of the City municipal district. The Bill was withdrawn before it reached the second reading, and Lord Elcho announced his intention of proceeding by Resolution. No suitable day was, however, available.

Municipality of London Bill, 1880. This Bill was prepared and brought in by Mr. Firth, Mr. Thorold Rogers, Mr. T. B. Potter, and others. It was read a first time on the 17th of June, but was not read a second time. This Bill creates a central, representative, municipal authority for the whole metropolis, to be called the "Municipality of London," and transfers to it all the powers and privileges of the Corporation of the City, the Metropolitan Board of Works, the Vestries and District Boards, and other bodies or persons exercising any municipal functions within the metropolis. It also provides that the Secretary of State, with the consent of the Local Government Board, may at any time transfer the powers of the Metropolitan Asylums Board to the new body. It creates the metropolis a county by the name of the County of London. It abolishes the vestries and district boards, and makes provision for the re-division of the metropolis into forty municipal districts. It applies the Municipal Corporations Acts generally to the Municipality of London, but saves to the new Corporation all the rights and privileges of the Corporation of the City which are not inconsistent with the provisions of those Acts.

The London Government Bill, 1884. This Bill was brought in by Sir William Harcourt, Sir Charles Dilke, the Attorney General, Mr. Hibbert, and Mr. George Russell. It was read a first time on the 8th of April, and the debate on the second reading came on on the 3rd of July. The debate was adjourned to the 4th and again to the 8th of July. After a long debate on the 8th, the debate was again adjourned, and the Bill was withdrawn on the 10th July. The Bill extends the area of the City of London and the County of the City of London, so as to include the whole metropolis; reforms the Corporation of London on the lines of the Municipal Corporations Acts, and transfers to the reformed Corporation, in addition to all the powers exercised by the old Corporation or the Commissioners of Sewers within the City, the powers and duties of the Metropolitan Board of Works, the vestries and district boards, the justices of Middlesex, Surrey, and Kent, within the metropolitan area, the burial boards, the Commissioners for Public Baths and Washhouses, Public Libraries and Museums, any Commissioners for paving, lighting, watching, and cleansing, in any part of London, and certain of the duties and liabilities and property of the Commissioners of Works.

It applies most of the provisions of the Municipal Corporations Act, 1882, to London; provides for the division of London into Municipal districts, and the election of district councils. The Lord Mayor is to be a fit person, qualified to be a Common Councillor; the Queen must approve his appointment as at present. He is to be by virtue of his office a Common Councillor and a Justice of the Peace, but with no larger power than that of a single Justice. His term of office is one year, but he is eligible for re-election. The Common Council is to fix his allowances or remuneration; and, subject to the provisions of the Bill, he is to have all the powers and precedence of the former Lord Mayors of London. The Council may elect a Deputy Mayor from among the Common Councillors, and may pay him; he is to be a Justice of the Peace for London during his year of office. The Aldermen of the Corporation of London at the passing of the Act are to hold office till the 1st May, 1885. After that date the title of Alderman is abolished, but the existing Aldermen of the City will continue to be Justices of the Peace for the County of London. The Common Council is to consist of 240 members exclusive of the Lord Mayor, but power is given to alter the number both of Common and District Councillors by a scheme confirmed by the Queen in Council. The control of the City Police is given to the new Corporation, but the Metropolitan Police remain under the Home Office. The purposes to which the City Fund may be applied are wider than in the case of other Municipal Corporations, and include the entertainment of distinguished persons, contributing to public charitable objects, and the maintenance of certain schools. The office of Recorder is continued, and provision is made for the appointment of Deputy-Recorders, one of whom is to be the Common-Serjeant. The Lord Mayor, Aldermen, Judge of the City of London Court, and the Dean of Arches, cease to be Judges of the Central Criminal Court: but the Recorder and Deputy-Recorders are to be included in the Commission. The Common Council is to submit a Bill to Parliament for dealing with the Mayor's Court; and the City of London Court is transferred to the Commissioners of Works and becomes a County Court. The Metropolitan Police Courts Acts are extended to the City, and the justice rooms at the Guildhall and Mansion House become Police Courts.

4. The new authorities alluded to on p. 13 are (1) the Managers of the London Children Asylum District, which was proposed by the Local Government Board in January, 1897, for the purposes of the relief of certain classes of children chargeable to London unions and parishes. The President of the Local Government Board denied that this was a new authority, but it was to consist of fifty-five members elected by the Guardians of the unions and parishes of London. And (2) the Metropolitan Water Board, proposed by the Government Bill of 1896, which was to consist of sixteen members elected by the London County Council—two by the Common

Council of the City of London, two by the Middlesex County Council, two by the Essex County Council, two by the West Ham Corporation, one by each of the other Metropolitan Counties, one by the Thames Conservancy, and one by the Lea Conservancy.

5. The position assumed by Exeter (p. 17) is discussed very fully by Mr. Freeman in *History of Norman Conquest*, vol. iv. pp. 138 *et seq.*

6. The districts into which England and Wales is divided (p. 19) are classified into two groups, Urban and Rural—a classification which exists wholly for the purpose of determining the sanitary functions which they are to administer. The extent of the district jurisdiction is shown in the following table:—

	No.	Area in Acres.	Population.
Urban Districts	709	2,181,995	5,713,888
Rural Districts	575	34,045,030	8,107,021
Total Districts	1,284	36,227,025	13,820,909

The rest of the country is comprised in the following:—

	No.	Area in Acres.	Population.
County of London	1	75,442	4,232,118
County Boroughs	64	347,889	7,588,536
Municipal Boroughs . . .	238	667,529	3,360,962
	303	1,090,860	15,181,616
Total England and Wales . . .	1,587	37,317,885	29,002,525

7. The process by which the Police District was formed is very instructive in connection with the subject discussed on page 19. Mr. F. W. Maitland, in his volume on *Justice and Police* in the "English Citizen Series," p. 98, says:—"From the institutions, distinctive of London proper, we pass to one which was long distinctive of 'the Metropolis,' for as yet we have no better name for the vast town which has agglomerated itself outside the City walls. This town, we must remember, was in the eye of the law no town; it had no legal being; it was but a collection of townships, and manors,

parishes, and extra parochial places, which owned no common ruler, save King and Parliament. Geography and remote history had done their worst for the Metropolis: the Commissions of the Peace for Middlesex, Surrey, Kent, and Essex, converged on the disorderly mass, while separate Commissions for Westminster and the Liberty of the Tower confounded confusion. Unity of action was impossible, the individual Magistrate was not controlled by the spirit of corporate magistracy, and metropolitan Justice and Police fell into bad ways. In the last century there arose men who gained the bad name of 'trading Justices,' and made a profit of their powers by the taking of fees. To put an end to this, rather than to do anything else, was the object of a series of statutes which ended by giving us professional Magistrates and a new police force under the control of Royal Commissioners and the Home Secretary. In 1792 seven 'public offices,' which came to be called 'police offices,' were established; at each of which, three Justices of the Peace, appointed by the King and commissioned for both Middlesex and Surrey, were to attend daily. All fees taken by them were to be paid to a receiver, and no other Justice was to take fees within a certain large district. Out of these fees, or, if they would not suffice, out of the Consolidated Fund, each of the twenty-one Justices was to be paid a salary of £400, while over the provision of buildings, and so forth, the Home Secretary was to have a control. An Act of 1800 established an eighth police office (or rather a ninth, for the Bow Street Office has an earlier history); and the three paid Justices ('Special Justices' they were called) of this Thames Police Office were to be commissioned for Middlesex, Surrey, Kent, Essex, Westminster, and the Tower. These Acts were only temporary, but they were repeatedly re-enacted with improvements. The salary of these Justices, or 'Police Magistrates,' as the later Acts called them, slowly grows from £400 to £1,500; the hours of attendance on the other hand are shortened; at first they are 10 to 8, afterwards 10 to 5. What this indicates is the great change which during this period is making the duties of the Justice in criminal cases more and more judicial. These paid Justices were seldom lawyers; it is first in 1839 that the King's choice is confined to barristers of seven years' standing. One of their chief duties had been to appoint and control a small band of paid constables attached to each office. Even in 1829, when 'a new police force' for 'the Metropolitan Police District' was formed, this was done by establishing in Westminster one more police 'office,' provided with two paid Justices of the Peace, who, under the Home Secretary, were to rule the new constabulary. In 1839 these two Justices receive the new name of 'Commissioners of Police of the Metropolis,' the judicial and executive duties comprised in the old conservation of the peace fall apart, and we are left with learned Magistrates and gallant Commissioners."

8. The Districts which are not local districts in the sense of Local Government (p. 20) are as follows:—

Sewerage Districts—
Richmond.
West Kent.
Darenth Valley.
Wisbech and Walsoken.
Upper Stour Valley.
Stourbridge.
Birmingham, Tame and Rea.
Haslingden and Rawtenstall.
Accrington and Church.
Clayton-le-Moors and Great Harwood.

River Districts—
Thames.
Lea.
Mersey and Irwell.
Ribble.
West Riding Rivers.

Most of the Port Sanitary Authorities, all the Commissioners of Sewers, the Drainage, Embankment, and Conservancy Boards, and the Fishery Conservancy Boards.

9. The difference between true localities, that is, localities formed by common interests and afterwards obtaining governing powers, and quasi localities, that is, localities formed for the purpose of administering central laws (p. 20), is perhaps best illustrated by an example. I therefore quote the following passage:—"Local Government is a word which requires special explanation in the case of Spain. Her whole life has been made to depend upon the Central Government, and, in consequence, every portion of this life is organized

according to the principles on which the constitution of Spain is framed. The source of political life arises from the constitution; and each political convulsion, re-modelling as it does the constitution on the principles of a new scheme, produces, with a new code, a fresh series of organic laws for the provinces and towns, called, after the old Roman names, provincias and municipios. Local life and Local Government mean, consequently (in Spain), a portion of the Central Government; therefore they afford no trace, either of special principles, special organization, or the remains of old institutions. There is nothing but Central Government modified and extended to comparatively local purposes" ("Local Government and Taxation," *Cobden Club Essays*, p. 338).

10. The importance of the proposition that the governing authority is only the trustee of the whole body of electors (p. 22) is shown in several ways. Thus, in a case tried before the Lord Chancellor, Lord Herschell, Lord Macnaghten, and Lord Morris, *The Churchwardens, etc., of Lambeth* v. *The London County Council*, the Lord Chancellor said that one sentence was sufficient to dispose of the case—namely, that the public, for whom the County Council were merely custodians or trustees, were not rateable occupiers, and that there was no beneficial occupation of the property whatever. (*The Times*, 20th July, 1897.)

11. The practice of allocating a portion of Imperial taxation to the purposes of local taxation (p. 23) was commenced in 1833 by a grant towards the cost of the Metropolitan Police, and it has been extended from time to time by grants towards the following services:—

    1835. Criminal prosecutions.
    1846. Teachers in poor law schools and poor law medical officers.
    1856. Police (counties and boroughs).
    1865-6. Metropolitan Fire Brigade.
    1870. Education.
    1873-4. Medical officers and sanitary inspectors.
    1874. Pauper lunatics.
    1875. Registration of births and deaths.
    1876. Industrial schools.
    1882. Disturnpiked and main roads.
    1891. Educational—fee grant.

Up to 1888 these grants were made direct to the authorities who spent the money, and were a fixed proportion of the amount spent, being subject to a check by the Imperial authority by means of a proper system of audit and by provisions for disallowances. In 1888 a very important departure was made in the method of making all the grants, except that for education. In the first place, certain definite duties locally collected were allotted to the counties in which they were collected; and, secondly, a certain stated proportion of the probate duty—now estate duty—and of the beer and spirit duties was allotted among the counties, the basis of apportionment being not the expenditure of the counties upon any given service, but the total grants made by the Government to the local authorities within the counties in one particular year, 1887. Since this considerable change in the principle upon which grants from the Imperial exchequer to local taxation took place, further changes have been adopted or are proposed by the Government to be adopted. These changes consist in throwing certain charges upon the local taxation account of the Imperial exchequer and deducting them from the amount set apart to be apportioned upon the principle of 1888. Thus, the cost of inspection for swine fever, which is undertaken and paid for by the Government, is deducted from the amount to be apportioned to the counties, and thus becomes a charge upon the counties, although indirectly made. Further, there are the provisions of the Agricultural Rates Act.

LECTURE II

12. The number of instances of counties and parishes having detached portions situated at some distance from the main area, and divided from that area by territory of other counties or parishes (p. 40), is very large. The schedule to the Act, 2 and 3 Will. IV., cap. 64, sets out the counties which had detached portions situated away from the main county area.

13. The elucidation of the tribal history of Britain (p. 43) has received almost unexpected light from Mr. Willis-Bund's remarkable researches in his recent book on the *Celtic Church in Wales*. Mr. Skene's *Celtic Scotland*, Sir Henry Maine's *Early History of Institutions*, and Mr. Seebohm's *Tribal System in Wales* are well-known works. My own contribution is contained in a communication before the British Association at Liverpool in 1896 on *Fire Rites and Ceremonials*.

14. The shires not included among the local government areas, the counties (p. 44), are very interesting fragments of the ancient constitution, and they are more frequently mentioned in earlier writers than is generally supposed. Thus Leland tells us that " Lancastreshire conteineth five litle shires " (*Itinerary*, vii. p. 44).

15. The early names of the shires (pp. 44-5) in connection with the tribes who formed them are discussed in Kemble's *Saxons in England*, vol. i., chapter 3. Palgrave's *English Commonwealth*, vol. i., p. 48, and the *Census Report* of 1851 (vol. i., pp. lvi.–lxxxii.), also give very valuable information. In addition to the ordinary chronicle sources of information referred to by these authorities, the student should consult a valuable reprint of " The Shires and Hundreds of England," published by the Early English Text Society in the *Old English Miscellany*, pp. 145-6.

16. The original of the Herefordshire record (p. 50) is printed in Hickes' *Dissertatio Epistolaris*, p. 4, in *Thesaurus Antiquitatum Septentrionalium*, vol. iii.

17. The original of the Pennenden Heath record (p. 52) is printed in Wilkins' *Concilia Magnæ Britanniæ*, vol. i. pp. 323-324.

18. The power of outlawry (p. 63) is perhaps the most remarkable survival of tribal conditions that occurs, and it would be difficult to account for its existence, except by the fact that the shire is descended from the tribe—was the tribe expressed in later terms. It existed with the primitive Russian mirs until the present year, when we are told that "on the advice of the Minister of the Interior, M. Goremykine, the Government have resolved to withdraw from the *mirs* the right to banish members of the village communities who offend against the laws and regulations that govern the administration of their common property and land."

The reader should consult Wallace's *Russia* (vol. i., 199), and Kovalevsky's *Modern Customs and Ancient Laws of Russia*.

19. The continuity of the site where the ancient shire-mote and the modern County Council of Kent meet (p. 64), is a very interesting point. Mr. Larking thus sums up the case : " Thither still the sheriff summons the freeholders to meet and nominate their knights of the shire. Thither are summoned, on all occasions, the men of Kent, to hold their meetings for public and political purposes. There is a lofty mound there at the meeting of the roads from Maidstone, now enclosed within the grounds of Foley House, which has a very suspicious look as having been the mote or hill on which the Gemote was held." (Larking's *Domesday of Kent*, Note No. 41, p. 160.)

20. This new liability of the county (p. 73) has already been put in force, as the following note will show :—

" At the Public Hall, Woking, an inquiry was opened under the Riot (Damages) Act, 1886, by representatives of the Surrey County Council. The notice in respect of the inquiry stated that a claim had been received 'from George Raggett, of Woking, for compensation amounting to £58 10s. for injury to, and destruction of, a freehold building at Bunker's Lane, Woking, of which he is the owner, by persons riotously and tumultuously assembled together on January 12th, 1897.' Colonel Tedcroft presided over the inquiry, and Mr. Fearon represented the claimant. It was stated that a building erected on freehold land near Woking was let at a rental of 3s. a week to a man who died in September, 1894. After that date the widow paid no rent, and as a result there were County Court proceedings and an ejectment order. On January 12th a number of persons assembled at the property, from which the widow had removed her furniture, and proceeded to demolish the premises. Some of the chief offenders were prosecuted, and sentenced at the assizes to terms of hard labour." (*Times*, 12th March, 1897.)

LECTURE III

21. On the Domesday possessions of the burghs (p. 81), Ellis' *Introduction to Domesday*, vol. i., pp. 190–210, may be consulted, but the subject wants special inquiry. Mr. Round has investigated the special case of Colchester in the *Antiquary*, vi., p. 97. Professor Maitland's criticism may be found in his *Domesday*, pp. 200-201.

22. In the case of Gloucester (p. 94) the Corporation possess a rent-roll, drawn up in 1455, by Robert Cole, a Canon of Llanthony Priory, near Gloucester. This roll is written in Latin, on parchment, and measures thirty-three feet in length by fifteen inches in width. It gives an account of every house in the borough, the

names of the owner and tenant, the tenant's trade, the amount of rent, the amount payable for landgavel rent, and, in many cases, an abstract of title from the time of Henry III. Each of the four main streets is taken in turn, the houses on each side of the street being given *seriatim* in separate columns, and then the side streets and lanes are similarly described. Between the columns a space is left to represent the roadway. In this space are curious drawings of the various churches, chapels, friaries, wells, the pillory, etc. The work is thus practically a survey and directory as well as a rent-roll of the city in 1455. Now this roll was not required for the purposes of taxation, as in the case of a modern valuation list; and it represents, therefore, the interest of the Corporation in the town property. Similarly, in other municipal towns, as, for instance, at Axbridge, in Somersetshire, there exists a vast accumulation of deeds relating to property in the town, and there is no explanation as to why the town should possess these deeds. The true explanation is, I am convinced, to be found in the early connection between the Corporation and the property of the town.

23. There are municipal boroughs in which to this day no rates are levied, owing to their possession of property (p. 94). This occurs in Ireland in Carrickfergus, Cashel, Drogheda, Kells, Clonakilty, Tuam, Belturbet, Callan, Fethard, and Kilkenny. The municipal revenue is derived in each of the first four cases from real property; in the next two, from tolls levied at markets and fairs; in the last four, partly from tolls and partly from property. The Corporation of Waterford and the Commissioners of Wicklow are possessed of sufficient income to render the levying of rates for ordinary municipal purposes unnecessary, the only rates levied being in connection with water supply. Many towns have a considerable revenue arising from property, market tolls, and other permanent sources of income (*Local Taxation, Ireland, Returns*, 1895, p. 15). Aldeburgh, in Suffolk, is an example in England.

24. Mr. Round has dealt with the subject of communal house demolition (p. 94) in his collection of studies published under the title of *Feudal England*. He says that the custom was limited to the Cinque Ports, and gives numerous parallels in Flanders and Northern France. But I think this is hardly so. The facts as I have collected them are as follows.

The Custumal of Sandwich contains the following item relative to the custom :—

"Si maior sic electus officium suum recipere noluit, primo et secundo et tercio monitus, tota communitas ibit ad capitale messuagium, si habuerit proprium, et illud cum armis omnimodo que poterit prosternat usque ad terram. . . . Similiter quicunque juratus fueret electus, et jurare noluerit simile judicium."

At Folkestone, if either the mayor or any of the jurats refused to assume their respective offices upon being elected, "the commons were to go and beat down their principal messuage" (*Report of the Record Commission*, 1837, p. 453). On the occasion of the election of bailiff at Hastings it was a law that "if the said bailiff be absent, or will not accept the charge, all the commoners shall go and beat down his chief tenement" (*Sussex Archæological Collections*, xii. 197). This clearly establishes the practice as an old Cinque Port law. Now let us turn to London. The assize of Henry II. states "that the house of the individual who harbours a heretic *shall be carried out of the town and burnt*" (Section 21). See Palgrave's *English Commonwealth*, vol. ii., p. clxxiii. There is the same principle underlying this and the Cinque Port custom. And if we turn to the Preston Guild Laws it receives curious confirmation. Every new burgess was obliged to erect his burgage within forty days (*Ancient Custumal of Preston*, Section 5); and the shortness of this period is explained by the fact noted by the authors of the *History of Preston Guild*, p. 47, Messrs. Dobson and Harland, that the houses "were formed of a framework of oak, and the interstices were filled with a sort of plaster formed of clay mixed with straw, reeds, or rushes. Each piece of wood in the framework was usually tenoned, fitted into a mortise, and fixed by a wooden peg. *The framework was put together by the builder before it was taken to the site.* When the old buildings facing the market-place were removed in 1855, much curiosity was excited by an examination of the framework, each tenon and mortise being numbered to correspond with each other, so that when the frame was placed on the site it had to occupy, the component parts could be as easily fitted to each other as when it was framed." This carrying of the framework to the site clearly explains the possibility of carrying houses out of the city of London, bearing in mind the evidence given by the assize of Fitzalwyne, first Lord Mayor of London, that the houses in the city were all thatched (*Liber Albus*, vol. i. p. 328), while from Stow we get a curious story:—In Throgmorton Street, Cromwell, Earl of Essex, built "one very large and spacious house," and pulled down the palings of the gardens adjoining, and enclosed them in his own grounds. Nor was this all. "My father," says Stow, "had a garden there, and a house standing close to his south pale; this house they loosed from the ground and bare upon rollers into my father's garden twenty-two feet ere my father heard thereof." These houses therefore were houses that could be moved.

25. The relationship of London to Middlesex illustrates the point alluded to on page 97, but it is one of those subjects which has not been properly worked out. The following notes suggest where such an inquiry might lead us. Fitzstephen, in the reign of Henry II., describes the garden ground, the arable lands providing plentiful corn like the rich fields of Asia, the pasture lands on the north, and the extensive forests, in which are wild beasts, bucks and does, wild boars and bulls (*Liber Custumarum*, i. 4); and I think we have a relic of this old municipal life beyond the walls in the surviving name of "Long Acre," one of the acre strips of the old common arable field. That this land belonged to the citizens in their corporate capacity and was utilized by them is incidentally proved by some curious entries in the *Liber Albus*, which contains a list of grants—concessio majoris et communitatis—among which extra-mural property is granted away with a free hand (*Liber Albus*, i. 552, "de domo vocata Bedlem extra Bysshopisgate, de domo extra Newgate, de quadam domo extra Crepulgate"), and then we have the instructive document "Memorandum de quadam placea terrae extra Crepulgate capta in manum civitatis." It is just possible that the tyrannical act of Henry III. may have given a great wrench to this state of things, for we learn that in 1265 he took all the "foreign" lands of the citizens into his hands, and foreign lands are those without the liberties (*Chronicles of the Mayors and Sheriffs*, p. 83).

Thus then it seems that the early municipal history of London tells us of a London outside the boundaries of the city itself, and that this extra-mural part of London municipal life falls in with the general tenor of English municipal history and the facts of English municipal boundaries. But there is something of a still wider area than this attached to old municipal life in London. The origin of Middlesex has generally, and on philological grounds only, been attributed to a tribe of the Middle Saxons, a tribe otherwise unknown to history. But a much more likely origin is that London and its *territorium* kept up a longer independence than other districts, and so divided the Saxons into South and East Saxons, the district itself being afterwards called Middlesex (Cf. *Journ. Anthropological Inst.*, vii. 305). This conjecture is confirmed when we come to apply the test of history. Thus, the charter of Henry I. confirms to the citizens "their chases to hunt as well and fully as their ancestors have had," a clause which clearly points to ancient prescriptive rights not dependent upon the chartered grants of the Norman sovereign, and so thorough-going a believer in Teutonic conquest as Mr. Green suggests that "Middlesex possibly represents a district which depended on London in this earlier [*i.e.*, 500-577], as it certainly did in a later time, and the privilege of the chase which its citizens enjoyed throughout the Middle Ages in the woodland that covered the heights of Hampstead and along the southern bank of the river as far as the Cray, may have been drawn from the rights of the Roman burghers" (*The Making of England*, 106, 107). Diocesan history almost everywhere in England is the key to much of the obscurer elements in the early history of English institutions (Stubbs' *Const. Hist.*, i. 225), and it is confirmatory of the origin of Middlesex from the *territorium* of London that the prebendal manors which have so long been in the hands of St. Paul's Cathedral were for the most part in Middlesex and occupied a belt of land extending from the very walls of London to the boundary of the county (Hale's *Domesday of St. Paul's*, p. iv.).

Looking a little closer into the municipal privileges of London, we find that they extended beyond the walls in all directions. The sheriff of London, it is well known, had jurisdiction over the county of Middlesex, and a curious record is extant showing how this was once attacked by Henry III., who "requested" the corporation to permit the "Abbot of Westminster to enjoy the franchise which the King had granted him in Middlesex in exchange for other liberties which the citizens might of right demand," but it was decided afterwards that "the sheriffs of London may enter all vills and tenements which the Abbot holds in Middlesex even unto the gate of his Abbey" (*Chronicles of the Mayors and Sheriffs*, pp. 16, 61). Southwark is an outer ward. Mile End, towards the east, was the gathering ground of the train-bands. Finsbury and

Smithfield, towards the north, were the play-grounds of the citizens. At Marylebone by the conduits the Lord Mayor had a banqueting-house (Maitland's *Hist. of London*, ii. 1373). Knightsbridge, to the west, seems to have marked the spot where the citizens deemed it proper to welcome guests within their boundaries, for in 1257 it is recorded that "upon the King approaching Westminster the mayor and citizens went forth to salute him, *as the usage is*, as far as Kniwtebrigge" (*Chronicles of the Mayors and Sheriffs of London*, p. 34), and in the regulations which govern the doings of Lorrainers, Knightsbridge, together with Stratford, Sandford, and Bolkette, are mentioned as the "four limits" (*Liber Custumarum*, i. 61 ; ii. 530).

LECTURE IV

26. The following passage from Palgrave is worth quoting to illustrate the position of the English township referred to on p. 113. "The earliest notices respecting the Teutonic townships are to be collected from the laws of the Salic Franks. A 'villa' was entirely the property of the inhabitants, and no stranger could settle within its boundaries, unless with the consent of the whole incorporation. Any one individual townsman could forbid the entrance of the new colonist upon the common fields of the sept. If after three warnings had been given, and thirty nights had elapsed, the intruder continued contumacious, he was summoned to the 'Mallum,' or Court, and in default of appearance the Gravio proceeded to the spot, and by force expelled the occupant from the purpresture which he had made. But it is important to remark that the freedom of the community might be legally acquired by an uncontradicted residence (of twelve months)."—Palgrave, *English Commonwealth*, i. 83.

27. The famous example of Ditmarsh (p. 122), situated between the Frisians of the great confederation and the Northern Frisians of Holstein, is explained by Mr. G. B. Williams in *Archæologia*, vol. xxxvii., pp. 371-390. The great emigrating tribe from Friesland, the Vogdemannen, established itself in two marks on the seashore, calling themselves the North and South Vogdemannen. The emigrating tribe from Saxony settled in the midst of the country in two other marks, which afterwards received the names of North and South Hamme. In later times a fifth district was added—the Meldorper

Döfft. Such was the original settlement by Ditmarsh—a settlement made by men who only did not become English as we understand the term because they did not follow their brethren to Britain, a settlement simply and thoroughly an agricultural community, with peasants alike for their aristocracy and their democracy, with peasants for their soldiers and peasants for their statesmen.

European politics, however, soon endeavoured to force themselves upon this primitive state of things. The first step was the granting of the land to the Bishop of Bremen, who, without interfering with the internal organization of the people, became lord of the unappropriated waste lands, somewhat analogous, says Mr. Williams, to our Lord of the Manor.

The account of the old government of the county as quoted by Mr. Williams from Neocorus is as follows:—" The old Ditmarsh government was arranged in the following manner: there were in every parish 'the sixteens,' as they were called; amongst them were two schlüter, who were also obliged to administer the possessions of the Church as churchwardens. They held their consultations weekly throughout the year, and if anybody intended to go to law he was to appear before this tribunal, and he demanded that the party of whom he complained should also appear before the court; upon that one of the neighbours of the defendant was obliged to summons him. When the two parties had arrived, and the complainant and the defendant had been heard, the court of law pronounced sentence. If any one was not satisfied, he might appeal from the sixteens to the whole parish. In small parishes there were sixteen, in the larger ones twenty-four kerknemedes. All appeals were brought before the parish, which decided. Usually the kerknemedes were judges in matters of debt, the schlüter were the judges of the scoundrels, thieves, and robbers. If the schlüter of a parish was not strong enough, they called to their aid all the other schlüter of the county to assist in the binding and the burning, which were the punishments of the whole land." The parish nemedes were the sworn representatives elected for life by the community of each parish from the most worthy and well-to-do of their members.

From their body the juries were invariably chosen, and on that account a jury was called a nemede (named). The schlüter were two officers annually chosen from the nemedes, whose business it was to convene the nemedes, to preside over the juries, and to give effect to their verdict, to superintend the apportioning of the land by lot, to direct all military affairs and to take charge of all roads, bridges and dykes. Up to this time each parish had been in effect a kind of separate republic, and had occasionally made separate treaties with foreigners, which were sealed with the parish seal. Each geschlecht, or bund, of perhaps two hundred families had its natural elder or head, and there was evidently some jurisdiction exercised over the members, as the family was responsible for their conduct. Beyond all this, moreover, was the supreme government invested in the "advocatus, milites, consules et tota communitas terræ thetmarsi." The milites were the natural heads of the geschlechts or races, and they rose to their condition without any rivalry, and sat as counsellers with the geschwornen of the different parishes.

LECTURE V

28. The documents to consult on the subject of pawnbroking (p. 145) are *Reports from Her Majesty's representatives on the system of pawnbroking in various countries,* 1894 (C—7559); *Report of the select committee of the House of Commons on Pawnbrokers,* 1870; "How to Municipalize the Pawnshops" by Robert Donald (*New Review*, December, 1894); and a printed speech at the London County Council by Mr. W. H. Dickinson on the municipalization of pawnbroking.

29. Water supply is an important service (p. 154). Of the 64 county boroughs in England and Wales, 43 have the water supply in their own hands, and 1—namely, Middlesborough—is supplied, together with the municipal borough of Stockton, by a joint water board. In 12 of these 44 cases the waterworks were originally constructed by the corporation, and in the remaining 32 they have been purchased from companies. Of the 20 county boroughs without a municipal water supply, 1—namely, the borough of Bootle—is supplied by the Liverpool Corporation, thus leaving 19 county boroughs supplied by private companies. Of the 32 cases of purchase, 23 were purchased by agreement settled before the passing of an Act, and afterwards embodied in or confirmed by the Act; 4 were purchased by agreement under Acts in which, failing agreement, arbitration was to be under the Lands Clauses Consolidation Acts; 2 (together with two of the Liverpool companies) were purchased by arbitration under the Lands Clauses Consolidation Acts; 1 was purchased by arbitration under special terms mentioned in the

Act; and 2 (Manchester and St. Helens) were settled by agreement after the passing of an Act authorizing purchase. There are in England and Wales, besides the county boroughs, 240 municipal boroughs, including the City of London. It is not easy to find out exactly what has happened in all of these cases with regard to water supply. So far as information is obtainable, it would appear that the water supply is in the hands of the corporation in 117 of these boroughs; 7 are supplied by joint water boards or committees, and 1 is supplied by another corporation. In the great majority of these cases the works were originally constructed by the corporation, but there is information that in 25 cases the works of companies were purchased.

30. The following Memorandum prepared for the use of the select committee on burial grounds, by Mr. W. P. Byrne, 13th July, 1897, gives a very useful summary of the subject of burial grounds (p. 160). This Memorandum does not apply to cemeteries under the Public Health Interments Act, which is administered entirely by the Local Government Board, but relates mainly to churchyards and burial grounds and additions to churchyards provided under the Burial Acts or the Church Building Acts. With regard to churchyards the freehold is in the incumbent, but the parishioners have the right of burial therein, and the management of the churchyard is vested, on behalf of the parishioners, in the churchwardens jointly with the incumbent. The minister and churchwardens have a discretion in what part of the churchyard the parishioner shall be buried, and even an alleged custom for the inhabitants of a parish to bury as near as possible to their ancestors is bad. Complaints occasionally reach the Home Office from parties who consider themselves prejudiced by the selection of the site for their relatives' graves, especially in cases of interment under the Act of 1880; but the Secretary of State has no authority in the matter.

If an addition to a churchyard is made by public subscription or private benefaction he may be, and usually is, vested in trustees, to be held and used in the same manner as an existing churchyard, and in such cases the additional land is, it is believed, usually consecrated under the Consecration of Churchyards Act, 1867.

Burial grounds may be provided by burial boards, town councils, and urban district councils acting as burial boards, by joint burial committees under the Local Government Act of 1894, by parish councils acting in execution of the Burial Acts, or by companies acting under statutory powers. Except in the last case, such burial grounds are generally provided by means of loans raised from the Public Works Commissioners or others with the sanction of the Treasury or of the Local Government Board. Power to take lands compulsory for burial purposes is given to the Ecclesiastical Commissioners by the Church Building Acts, to parish councils by Section 9 of the Local Government Act, 1894, and to district councils by the Public Health Interments Act of 1879.

Before the Local Government Act, 1894, it was possible under the very wide powers conferred by the Burial Acts for almost any area which was not a merely fortuitous collection of houses, but had a vestry or meeting in the nature of a vestry, to appoint a burial board and provide itself with a burial ground. And as a matter of fact grounds were in a large number of cases provided for ecclesiastical areas with but slight reference to the civil parishes.

But now in every rural parish the parish meeting, exclusively, has the power of adopting the Burial Acts for that parish. When the Acts have been adopted by the parish meeting, the parish council, if any, will be the authority for the execution of the Acts; in parishes having no parish council the parish meeting can only act as the authority if specially authorized by the county council, and, if not so authorized, must appoint a burial board under the Acts.

And with regard to ecclesiastical parishes or districts made up of more than one or portions of more than one civil parish, notwithstanding such a district may have had a churchyard or burial ground in common for the use of the district, or its ratepayers have customarily met in one vestry for purposes common to all, the vestry or meeting in the nature of the vestry can no longer (since the Local Government Act, 1894, came into force) proceed under the Burial Acts. A burial ground can only be provided for such a parish by the separate civil parishes or portions of civil parishes (if such portions are portions which under the Burial Acts and Section 7 (4) of the Local Government Act, 1894, have the power) adopting the Acts severally and concurring in providing a burial ground in common.

Where the Burial Acts were, on the day on which the Local Government Act, 1894, came into force, in part only of a rural parish, the burial board or the parish meeting for that part may transfer the powers, duties, and liabilities of the board to the parish council, subject to any conditions with respect to the execution thereof by means of a committee as the board or parish meeting may think fit.

And further the county council, on the application of a parish council, may by order alter the boundaries of the area which was under any burial board on the day on which the Local Government Act, 1894, came into force.

But in urban districts it is still the case that a vestry or meeting of the nature of a vestry of a parish, whether poor law or ecclesiastical, or of a district for which such meetings have customarily been held, can, with the consent of the urban district council, appoint a burial board and provide a burial ground. It is possible, therefore, in urban districts to give effect to the desire which is not unfrequently shown to follow the ecclesiastical lines of division for burial purposes even where the ecclesiastical and civil boundaries are distinct. It may be considered doubtful whether the multiplication of separate rating areas which this involves should be encouraged or permitted; but there is evidence in the Home Office that the wish to adopt ecclesiastical divisions for burial purposes, in spite of their clashing with civil divisions in a very awkward manner, is not uncommon. For example, an application has quite recently been received for approval of the setting up of a Burial Board for an ecclesiastical district which consists of a part of a rural parish (civil) and a small portion of a municipal borough. The Home Office was advised that such a Board could not legally be constituted; and no doubt the general tendency of the Act of 1894 will be to cause burial districts to coincide with civil divisions. And this tendency will not be substantially removed by the powers given by the Act to parish councils to unite for purposes of common interest, as, *e.g.*, the provision of a burial ground; because there is no direct power given to a parish council to unite with the parish meeting of a parish which has no council, nor with a burial board.

31. The importance of efficient locomotive service (p. 163) is in respect of (1) the means of intercommunication between different parts of a locality for business and recreative purposes; (2) the housing of the working classes; (3) the carrying out of road improvements; (4) the provision of cheap and satisfactory means of transit of food and other products.

The Corporation of Folkestone are so interested in the South Eastern Railway service that they advertise its advantages to intended purchasers of property in Folkestone. The evidence collected and published by the Royal Commission on Agriculture prove the importance of Light Railways to localities. Many producers express their opinion that they are still most unfairly handicapped in competition with the foreign producers for the supply of the home markets, by reason of the reduced preferential rates conceded by the railway companies to the latter. As one witness forcibly put it, the struggling fruit-grower in Kent has to suffer the mortification of seeing foreign fruit carried by the railway past his farm at rates which would not be conceded to him, and of finding his produce, in consequence, undersold in the London market.

The Royal Commission elicited further important evidence as to the extensive adoption of light railways in almost every country on the Continent, notably in Germany, Belgium, France, Italy, and Hungary, and in the vicinity of large towns, for the cheap and expeditious distribution of agricultural products and the encouragement and development of agricultural enterprise.

The description given of the Belgian system may be referred to as more or less typical. There are 67 light railways, from 2 to 35 miles each in length, in the neighbourhood of most of the principal towns. The capital was supplied as follows:—

By the state to the extent of 27 per cent.
By the provinces to the extent of 28 per cent.
By the communes to the extent of 41 per cent.
By the public to the extent of 4 per cent.

The charge is as low as from 7 to 13 centimes per ton per kilometre for ordinary traffic, equivalent to $1·1d.$ and $2·03d.$ per ton per mile. There is also a special rate under which four tons are carried all distances for $1s.\ 2\frac{1}{2}d.$, or for $1\frac{1}{2}d.$ per kilometre, equivalent to about $2\frac{1}{2}d.$ per mile. Another special charge is $5d.$ per ton for all distances, or 4 centimes per kilometre, equivalent to about $·64d.$ per mile. These railways run alongside the main roads; they carry passengers as well as goods, and farmers travelling as passengers are allowed to take with them, free of charge, their small produce for sale in the towns.

32. The power of local authorities in early days with reference to buildings (p. 169) is hardly appreciated. Mr. Clifford, in his *History*

250   NOTES AND ILLUSTRATIONS

of Private Legislation (1. 29–30), states that in the reign of Henry VIII. a series of Acts were passed giving remarkable powers to municipal authorities. The wars of succession had probably led to some confusion of ownership in towns. Country gentlemen, too, had become unwilling or, through want of means, unable to maintain their ancient residences in the chief provincial centres. The result was, in the year 1540, "that many beautiful houses of habitation" had "fallen down, decayed, and at this day . . . do lie as desolate and vacant ground," while other houses were feeble and like to fall, and pits, cellars and vaults were uncovered and dangerous (27 Henry VIII. cap. 1 ; 32 Henry VIII. cap. 18 ; 33 Henry VIII. cap. 36). Municipalities complained, with reason, that these ruined mansions were "a hindrance and impoverishment" to them; that the abandoned sites became no man's land, disturbing to the peace of the community. Parliament listened to these representations, and prescribed a certain period within which owners should restore their houses. In their default the lords of whom the land was holden were allowed a further time to do so. If they, too, failed, local authorities might enter and do all necessary work, and, adds Mr. Clifford, "every considerable provincial town in England was thus dealt with."

33. The authority to consult on docks (p. 175) is Mr. L. F. Vernon-Harcourt's *Harbours and Docks*, 1885, 2 vols. It deals with their physical features, history, construction, equipment, maintenance, and gives statistics as to their commercial development, and very valuable plans.

LECTURE VI

34. The important principle of taxation according to benefit (p. 189) is illustrated by a long series of Acts. Thus special rates are leviable for bridges, shire halls, etc., over particular areas in certain cases—1530–1, 22 Henry VIII. cap. 5, bridges. 1815, 55 George III. cap. 143, bridges. 1826, 7 George IV. cap. 63, shire halls, etc. 1827, 7 and 8 George IV. cap. 31, damage by rioters. 1852, 15 and 16 Victoria, cap. 81, county rate in a divided parish. See *Two Memorandums on Local Government* of S. Whitbread, M.P., and W. Rathbone, M.P. (ii. 19).

Sewerage statutes are all upon the principle of benefit. A statute of Henry VI. (1427) authorized the Crown to grant commissions to make surveys, etc., and to inquire into annoyances resulting from ditches, gutters, etc., and by whose default caused, with power to distrain for reparations, "so that none should be spared that might receive benefit or defence, commodity or safeguard." This statute was followed by 23 Henry VIII. cap. 5 (1531). And there were also special statutes for the metropolis—3 and 4 Edward VI. cap. 8 (1549); 13 Elizabeth, cap. 9 (1571); 3 James I. cap. 4 (1605); 2 William and Mary, cap. 8 (sess. 2), (1691); 7 Ann, cap. 10 (1706).

Under these statutes Special Courts of Sewer Commissioners were established. As courts they could bind by their decrees property in fee or even entailed property, and by Act of Ann (1706) could sell the property if need be to enforce their decrees.

It was settled law that unless all benefited were assessed to the cost of the work the rate or decree for assessment was bad; to such an extent was this pushed that it was bad if the assessment did not include the King's land. None were to be spared that received benefit, even if the benefit were not immediate (Smith *v.* Wilson, 3 H. and E., 248).

The assessment was regarded in the nature of a betterment or improvement on the fee of the land (Smith *v.* Humble, 15 C. B., 330), and became a first charge, not on the occupier, but on the property in the nature of an encumbrance, the tenant having a right of deduction (Palmer *v.* Erith, 14 Mees and W., 428).

The sewer rate benefits property and is payable by the landlord, whether the property is tenanted or not (Holborn and Finsbury Sewers Act, 18 George III. cap. lxvi. p. 8, and the Surrey and Kent Sewers Act, 49 George III. cap. 183, sec. 36, p. 8). The Holborn Act states that it "shall be deemed and taken to be a charge upon the premises." It was levied upon the area benefited or upon the property benefited :—

Area Benefited.—See Surrey and Kent Sewers Act, 49 George III. cap. 183, sec. 45, p. 8, Metropolitan Sewers Act, 1848, 11 and 12 Victoria, cap. cxii. secs. 34 and 76, p. 9, and minute of the Metropolitan Commissioners of Sewers, issued thereunder, creating a new district in the Metropolitan district of Fulham and Hammersmith, p. 10.

Property Benefited.—See Westminster Sewers Act, 4 and 5 William IV. cap. xcvi. sec. 6, p. 11, Marylebone Streets Act, 53 George III. cap. cxxi. sec. 81, p. 12.

The area benefited had no relationship to parish boundaries, but consisted solely of the area of benefit. The unit to govern the liability was that of area of benefit, and sec. 81 of Metropolitan Commissioners of Sewers Act, 11 and 12 Victoria, cap. cxii., treated charge or rate on the same footing.

The 3 and 4 William IV. cap. 22, is the first Act that established differential rating in proportion to benefit derived, and conferred those powers on bodies other than commissioners of sewers—the rating proceeding on the principle of receiving benefit or avoiding damage.

By sec. 38 of the Land Drainage Act, 1861, a distinction is drawn between rating for improvements in old and in new works, and makes the cost of new works exceeding £1,000 and of all improvements in old works a special rate and a tax on owners.

Rating, according to the evidence of experts given before the select committee on conservancy boards (371 of 1877), should be according to benefit conferred or damage averted by improvements. Ridley (Enclosure Commissioner, Qn. 67)—"If I went down and said, 'Now this district has derived benefit, we will say, to the extent of £100 a year,' I would charge them for that, but if they are able to prove on appeal that they have not derived any benefit at all, this rate would be quashed." Mr. Speaker (Peel), Qn. 349—"It appears to me that the taxation should be spread over all, recognising the fact that the tax ought to be as proportionate as the damage averted is proportionate, or as the benefit received is proportionate." Mr. Brendell, C.E., Doncaster, Qn. 1128—1129—"All lands that would benefit by the improvement of the river should pay a contribution to meet the general improvement in proportion to the benefit received to be determined by an expert." Mr. Williams, Engineer of the Severn Navigation Commission, Qn. 1620—Mr. Tweedtown, Clerk of the City of Lincoln, Qn. 1911—"My idea is that they ought all to be rated, but of course there ought to be a sliding scale according as they are respectively benefited." Mills (land agent, Derwent), Qn. 2315—" I would most decidedly tax them according to the benefit which they are supposed to receive." Hawkins (Town Clerk of Oxford), Qn. 2760—2761—Sir John Hawkshaw (Civil Engineer), Qn. 2795—"I would rate the district in proportion to the benefit that it received as nearly as practicable; it is difficult sometimes to apportion the benefit with precision, and my proposition embraces to some extent those who occasion the floods as well as those who suffer from them."

Public and General Benefits and Assessments.—Will be found in cases under the Irish Cess Act, 1836, which directs collateral benefits to be taken into account as regards roads; under the Land Drainage Act, 1861, and Estate Improvements Act, 1864, in England; the Artizans' and Labourers' Dwelling Act, 1868, the Housing of the Working Classes Acts, 1885 and 1890, and the report of the Royal Commission on the Housing of the Working Classes, see post pages 16–23.

Paving Benefits and Assessments.—Rates were levied under these Acts upon the houses situated in the roads paved or repaired, and not upon other property in the parish. Local Acts—Bethnal Green, 33 George III. cap. 88, sec. 50 and 53; Southwark, 6 George III. cap. 24, sec. 51; Westminster, 11 George III. cap. 22 [p. 612]. A judgment of the Court of Queen's Bench, on the construction of sec. 159 of the Metropolis Local Management Act, 1855, laid down in the case of the London Docks that the area covered with water, and deriving in consequence no benefit from certain local charges, was not liable to be assessed for such benefits.

Lighting, Watching, etc., Benefits and Assessments.—These rates were levied according to benefits conferred, and if none were conferred no assessment was to be imposed (Hampstead Act). In some cases the Acts directly laid down these principles, and gave no other directions for assessing the benefits (Stoke Newington Act and Hampstead Act).

In other cases the rates were levied according to benefits conferred, and the Acts defined the limit of area, instead of leaving it open to the assessing authority to ascertain the nature and extent of the benefit, and directed that only properties within a certain distance of the road, lighted, watered or watched, were to be considered as deriving benefits, and in consequence liable to rate or assessment.

As illustration of rates levied upon houses in the roads which were lighted, etc., or upon houses within a certain distance of the roads in Shoreditch, Camberwell, Hampstead, trustees were enabled to rate all houses, etc., situated by the sides of the roads lighted or within two hundred yards thereof. In the case of Lambeth, it was limited to 500 yards; and in another case in Hampstead, it was limited to 100 yards.

Street Improvements, Benefits and Assessments.—The Act 13 and 14 Charles II. cap. 2, relating to the City of Westminster, passed before the Fire of London, contains a provision for charging owners of property with a capital sum as a rent in consideration of improvement to their property, it being declared that such property will receive much advantage in the value of their rent (see page 36). The 18 and 19 Ch. II. cap. 18, relating to the City of London, passed after the Fire of London, repeated the same principle, and Mr. Pepys in his Diary comments on the application of this principle. By the Act relating to St. John, Wapping (22 George III. cap. xxxv. sec. 27), the trustees are enabled to purchase buildings and lands and make and open streets in certain parts of the parish; section 36 enables the trustees to sell surplus lands; section 40 enables the trustees to make rates on houses, etc., within the streets and places opened and made under the Act, throwing one-third part of such rates upon the landlord, and the remaining two-thirds on the tenant; section 45 enacts that empty houses shall be rated at one-third and paid by the owners or proprietors; section 54 enables the trustees to borrow money by annuities, the security being the rates made on the intended new streets, and the annuities are charged upon such rates.

By the Act 28 George III. cap. 68 (Southwark) the commissioners are empowered to open, widen and improve certain streets, the particulars of which are set out in section 3, and by section 28 to levy an additional rate of 6*d*. upon the particular division in which the streets to be improved are situated, and by sections 31 and 32 these rates are charged upon the landlords.

35. The history of the Metropolitan Police Force is a very curious one, and worth noting from the point of view of development from local to national purposes (p. 200). It was established in 1829. The duties of the Horse Patrol and Thames Police were transferred to the Metropolitan Police in 1839. The employment of the Metropolitan Police in Her Majesty's yards and principal military stations outside the Metropolitan Police District was authorized in 1860.

In 1829 the district included Westminster and certain specified parts of Middlesex, Surrey and Kent, with power, by order in Council, to add all parishes, etc., in the above-named counties, and in Hertford and Essex of which any part is within 12 miles of Charing Cross.

In 1839 power was given by Order in Council to extend the district to include any part of the Central Criminal Court district, except the City of London and the Liberties thereof, and any part of any parish, etc., not more than 15 miles from Charing Cross.

An order in Council of 1840 enumerated the places which constitute the existing district. The district is made up as follows :—

    The County of London.
    The County of Middlesex.

In the County of Surrey the following parishes and places :— Addington, Banstead, Barnes, Beddington, Carshalton, Cheam, Chessington, Coulsdon, Cuddington, Epsom, Ewell (exclusive of Kingswood Liberty and including Worcester Park), Farley, Hamlet of Ham with Hatch, Hamlet of Hook, Kew, Kingston-on-Thames, Long Ditton, Maldon, Merton, Mitcham, Mordon, Mortlake, Moulsey (East and West), Petersham, Richmond, Sanderstead, Sutton, Thames Ditton (comprising the Hamlets of Clygate, Ember and Weston), Hamlet of Wallington, Warlingham, Wimbledon, and Woodmansterne.

The county borough of Croydon.

In the county of Herts the following parishes and places :— Aldenham (and Hamlet of St. Theobald, Aldenham), East Barnet, Bushey, Cheshunt, Chipping Barnet, Northaw, Ridge, Shenley and Totteridge.

In the county of Essex the following parishes and places :— Barking (including Chadwell, Great Ilford, and Ripple Wards), Chigwell, Chingford, Dagenham, East Ham, Little Ilford, Waltham Abbey and town (including the Hamlets of Holyfield, Sewardstone and Upshire), Wanstead and Woodford.

The county borough of West Ham.

In the county of Kent the following parishes and places :— Beckenham, Bexley, Bromley, Chislehurst, Crayford, Down, Erith, Farnborough, Foot's Cray, Hayes, Keston, Hamlet of Mottingham, North Cray, Orpington, St. Mary's Cray, St. Paul's Cray, and Wickham (East and West).

In 1844 the Police Acts were extended to Trafalgar Square.

Constables of the Metropolitan Police Force (specially sworn) act within the Royal Palaces and ten miles thereof.

Constables of the Metropolitan Police Force (a number directed by the Home Secretary and specially sworn) act within Her Majesty's dockyards and principal military stations, and within 15 miles thereof. They have full power within the yards and stations, but outside them only with respect to Crown property and persons subject to discipline.

The constables of the Metropolitan Police have full, but not exclusive, power in the counties of Berkshire and Buckinghamshire.

Also upon the river Thames within the counties of London, Middlesex, Surrey, Berkshire, Essex, and Kent, and within and adjoining to the City of London and the Liberties thereof, and in and on the creeks, inlets, waters, docks, wharfs, quays and landing places thereto adjacent. In those parts of the Thames which are beyond the district the powers are concurrent with those of the county or local police.

On any special emergency, at the request of the Lord Mayor, a Secretary of State may authorize Metropolitan Police to act within the City under their own officers.

Agreements to assist in special emergencies may be made with the authorities of other police forces.

The Commissioner is appointed by the Crown by warrant under the sign manual.

He is a justice of the peace for London, Middlesex, Surrey, Hertfordshire, Essex, Kent, Berkshire, and Buckinghamshire, although not qualified by estate. He may not act at general or quarter sessions, nor in any matter out of sessions, except for the preservation of the peace, the prevention of crimes, the detection and committal of offenders, and in carrying into execution the purposes of the Metropolitan Police Acts.

He can act as a justice only during the continuance of his appointment.

Under the directions of a Secretary of State he appoints the members of the Metropolitan Police Force.

He swears in members of the Metropolitan Police Force to act within the Royal Palaces and 10 miles thereof.

Under the direction of a Secretary of State he swears in members of the Metropolitan Police Force to act in Her Majesty's dockyards and principal military stations, and, subject to the approval of a Secretary of State, he may replace these by such additional constables as may be required.

He may, if he thinks fit, appoint additional constables, on the application and at the cost of private individuals, to keep the peace at any place within the Metropolitan Police District.

Subject to the approbation of a Secretary of State, he makes orders and regulations for the general government of the police force; the places of their residence; the classification, rank, and particular service of the several members; their distribution and inspection; the description of arms, accoutrements, and other necessaries to be furnished to them; and which of them shall be provided with horses for the performance of their duty; and all such other orders and regulations relative to the police force as he shall deem expedient for preventing neglect or abuse and for rendering the force efficient.

There are three Assistant Commissioners, who are appointed in the same manner as the Commissioner, have, as justices, the same powers, and are subject to the same disqualifications. Under his superintendence and control they aid the Commissioner in the discharge of his various duties, and perform acts and duties in the execution of the Police Acts as directed by orders and regulations made by the Commissioner with the approbation of a Secretary of State. Matters requiring to be done by the Commissioner may be done by an Assistant Commissioner nominated and as directed by a Secretary of State. In case of a vacancy in the office of Commissioner, or of his illness or absence, an Assistant Commissioner may act for him.

The Receiver of the Metropolitan Police is appointed by the Crown. He is subject to the same disqualifications as the Commissioner.

He receives all moneys applicable to the purposes of the Metropolitan Police; pays all salaries, wages, allowances, and other expenses incurred in carrying out the Police Acts; makes all contracts and disbursements necessary for purchasing or renting land or buildings, or for erecting, fitting up or repairing any buildings for the purposes of the Acts. All police property of whatever nature vests in him, and he alone can dispose of it under the direction of the Secretary of State.

He is a corporation sole and has an official seal.

He has wide powers of acquiring, holding, and disposing of land and other property.

He has compulsory powers of purchase for certain purposes, and may borrow for certain purposes on the security of the Police Fund, under the Local Loans Act, 1875, or from the London County Council.

All sales, purchases, or leases, etc., by the Receiver and the

S

raising of all loans are subject to the approval of a Secretary of State, and, in the case of loans, also of the Treasury.

He has power to sell unclaimed stolen property (which has been ordered by a magistrate to be delivered to him) after twelve months, and carry the proceeds to the Pension Fund.

He is the police authority for the Metropolitan Police District, to whom claims for compensation under the Riot (Damages) Act, 1886, are made. Claims are payable out of the Metropolitan Police Rate.

In addition to his duties in connection with the Metropolitan Police Force, the Receiver is also Receiver for the Metropolitan Police Courts.

Money is provided by annual votes of Parliament for the salaries of the Commissioner, the Receiver, and of two of the three Assistant Commissioners, but the allowances to the Commissioner and Assistant Commissioners for house rent, and the salary of the third Assistant Commissioner, are payable out of the Police Fund.

Parliament also provides money for the expenses of the employment of constables in Her Majesty's dockyards and military stations.

The annual sum provided for the expenses of the Metropolitan Police Force must not exceed 9$d.$ in the pound on the full annual value of all property rateable for the poor in the Metropolitan Police District.

Of this sum 5$d.$ is levied by a rate and 4$d.$ is paid out of the exchequer contribution. It is deducted from the amount payable under the Local Government Act, 1888, out of the local taxation account to the council of each county in the Metropolitan Police District in proportion to the amount raised by rate in the county, and is paid direct to the Receiver.

Fines for offences against the Metropolitan Police Acts recovered at courts other than Metropolitan Police Courts, and the proceeds of licenses for Hackney and stage carriages are also paid to the Police Fund.

In 1829 the maximum amount was fixed at 8$d.$, to be raised by rate.

In 1839 a sum not exceeding £20,000 was charged on the Consolidated Fund to meet the increased cost of the Metropolitan Police, caused by the transfer to them of the duties of the horse patrol and Thames police. This sum was transferred from the Consolidated Fund to annual votes by 17 and 18 Vict. c. 34.

In 1868 the maximum annual sum was increased to 9*d*., of which one-fourth was to be contributed by Parliament.

In 1875 the limitation of the parliamentary contribution to one-fourth was removed, and the amount contributed was subsequently equal to 4*d*. in the pound of the rateable value.

In 1888 the proportion of the expenses of the Metropolitan Police, which would have been contributed out of the Exchequer under the arrangement in force during 1887, was for the future charged upon the exchequer contribution.

Out of the Metropolitan Police Fund the Receiver pays:—

(1) The salary of the third Assistant Commissioner and the allowances for house rent made to the Commissioner and Assistant Commissioners.

(2) The salaries, wages, and allowances of persons belonging to the force.

(3) Any extraordinary expenses incurred in apprehending offenders and executing the orders of the Commissioner.

(4) Such sums as a Secretary of State may direct to be paid to members of the force as rewards for extraordinary diligence or exertion, or as compensation for injury received in performance of duty.

(5) All other charges and expenses which a Secretary of State shall direct to be paid for carrying the Police Acts into execution.

(6) Superannuation allowances, in accordance with the principles applicable to the Civil Service, of persons, not being constables, who are employed under the Commissioner or Receiver, and whose salaries are paid as part of the expenses of the force.

The Pension Fund was established in 1890. To this fund are paid:—

(*a*) An annual contribution of £150,000 under the Local Taxation (Customs and Excise) Act, 1890.

(*b*) A rateable deduction from pay, not exceeding $2\frac{1}{2}$ per cent. per annum.

(*c*) Stoppages during sickness and fines for misconduct as provided by regulations of force.

(*d*) The proceeds arising from the sale of unclaimed stolen goods.

(*e*) Fines imposed on constables, or for assaults on constables, and fines awarded to constables as informers.

(*f*) Sums arising from sale of cast-off clothing of force.

260 NOTES AND ILLUSTRATIONS

(*g*) Such proportion of any sum received on account of constables whose services have been lent in consideration of payment as the police authority may consider to be a fair contribution to the pension fund in respect of those constables.

(*h*) All dividends, etc., from investments of the pension fund.

Also, with consent of the authority having control of the fund to which the money would otherwise go :—

(*i*) Fees for pedlars and chimney sweeps' certificates.

(*j*) All fees payable to any constable of the force.

(*k*) Fines for offences under the Licensing Acts, 1872 and 1874.

This is summarized from Mr. Kemp's memorandum to the Royal Commission on London Government, 1894, *Appendix*, pp. 566-574.

LECTURE VII

36. The chaos in local taxation (p. 209) may be indicated by the entirely different methods adopted for the distribution of the grants from Imperial exchequer. These methods are—

(1) Licences, according to the amount collected within the county or county borough areas.

(2) Estate duties and beer and spirit duty, according to the grants actually made to the several local authorities within the county and county borough areas in the year 1887-8, but subject to special adjustment in one or two cases.

(3) Police pension grant, according to an arbitrary decision of Parliament founded on no basis beyond the immediate requirements of the police.

(4) Education grant, according to the results of education.

(5) According to the amount of taxation upon agricultural lands.

It is not only that the second and third of these methods are not good of themselves, but that they do not act as complements to the others. Thus places with the same burden of rates show as follows :—

	Ratio per cent. of rates to rateable value.	Ratio per cent. of Exchequer contributions to rateable value.	Proportion of local taxation borne by Exchequer contributions (per cent.).
Coventry.	22·15	4·60	17·20
Salford.	22·19	4·44	16·67
Ipswich.	22·38	4·45	16·58
Wigan.	22·50	3·93	14·87
Lincoln (county borough).	22·53	6·59	22·61
Middlesex.	22·59	4·38	16·24
Birmingham.	22·68	4·47	16·46
London.	22·41	3·37	13·07

The general result of this system is, that by the criterion of rateable value and of local taxation borne by Exchequer contributions London receives less than other places of the same burden of rates, and there is inequality throughout. Exclusive of the charge for education, a Londoner is relieved to the extent of about one-eighth of the amount he would have to pay in rates in the absence of Exchequer contributions, while an inhabitant of Salop or Westmoreland is relieved to the extent of nearly one-third. The ratios between London, county boroughs, and counties were, in 1893-4, as follows :—

	Ratio per cent. to total.		
	Rateable value.	Local taxation.	Exchequer contributions.
London.	20·74	24·95	18·45
County Boroughs.	20·41	25·11	22·03
Counties.	58·85	49·94	59·52
Total	100·00	100·00	100·00

37. The early system of taxation dealt with the counties, boroughs, and townships, and not with the individual taxpayer (p. 210). During the early years after the Conquest there is little information on this subject, because of the vast amount of the royal demesnes and the feudal dues which made service and work answer the purpose of taxation. But in the fourteenth century, the long wars with France and the change of economic and political conditions

produced a change in taxation, and the practice had been introduced of assessing the property of earls and barons, and the commonalty of counties and towns, to a twentieth, fifteenth, or tenth, according to requirements. But the assessment of 1332 produced a significant reform. Complaint had been made of oppression, extortion, and hardship, and to avoid these "a power was inserted in the writs issued for the assessment and collection of the tax, which amounted to a direction to the Royal Commissioners to treat with the communities of the cities and boroughs, the men of the townships and ancient demesne and all others bound to pay the fifteenth and tenth, and settle with them a fine or sum to be paid as composition for the fifteenth and tenth." The sum thus fixed was to be entered on the rolls as the assessment of the particular county, borough, or township; and counties, boroughs, and townships were required to assess and collect the amount upon and from the various individual contributors. Only in the case of a refusal to compound was the machinery of assessment and collection to be enforced. Henceforth, from 1334, the sum thus fixed by composition as for the fifteenth and tenth granted in 1334 was accepted as the basis of taxation; and on the grant of a fifteenth and tenth it was usual to declare that they should be levied in the ancient manner according to the ancient valuation (*Pipe Rolls*, ii. 447)—that is to say, that there should not be any new assessment, but that every particular county and town should pay the usual sum, a fifteenth for the county and a tenth for the city and borough. In process of time every particular county, city, and town assessed and collected the amount charged upon it by means of the method they found most convenient to them. When less than the sum for a full fifteenth and tenth was required, half a fifteenth and tenth was granted, and when a greater sum was required, it was granted under the name of two fifteenths and tenths, or as the case might be. This practice was continued, in spite of attempts to change it, down to modern times, and the Property Tax of William III., planted in the same soil, grew gradually to resemble the fifteenths and tenths in the form it attained of the fixed Land Tax of the eighteenth century. To the present day, at the distance of five centuries and a half, the consequences of the arrangement made in 1334 for the local assessment and collection of the fifteenth and tenth are clearly visible in England (Dowell's *Hist. of Taxation*, i. 86–88).

Counties, boroughs, and towns that kept the tax collector out of their territory, and handed over to the State certain proportional sums of the whole amount required, could apportion the burden upon the individual as they deemed it right that it should fall; that they exercised judgment in this matter is known from many examples.

38. The passage as to Remunerative and Non-Remunerative Rates (p. 215) in the Report on Scottish Local Taxation is as follows :—

In making a comparison of the amount of local rates falling upon urban and rural districts respectively, it is of importance that remunerative should, as far as possible, be distinguished from non-remunerative taxation—many of the new rates being of the nature of payment for benefits received, and not so much a burden as an investment—*e.g.*, lighting of streets, cleansing, paving, etc.

In distinguishing between non-remunerative and remunerative taxation I have followed the principle adopted in the English Local Taxation Returns some years ago, and have included, in the first class, sums levied for the maintenance of a police force (*i.e.*, the protection of life and property, and preservation of internal peace and order) and for the relief of the poor. All other rates have been placed in the second class.

The following Tables show the total amount of Remunerative and Non-Remunerative Rates raised in 1848 and 1893 :—

I. *Non-Remunerative Rates.*

Rates.	Urban Areas.		Rural Areas.	
	1848.	1893.	1848.	1893.
Poor Law	£180,771	£397,962	£284,096	£352,734
Police (Constabulary)	53,373	180,000	53,385	130,000
Total	234,144	577,962	337,481	482,734

II. *Remunerative Rates.*

Rates.	Urban Areas.		Rural Areas.	
	1848.	1893.	1848.	1893.
	£	£	£	£
Total Burgh Rates other than those required for Police	126,923	1,541,927	...	...
School Rates falling on Heritors	...	...	50,000	...
Ecclesiastical Rates falling on Heritors	...	...	30,000	34,563
Education Rates under Act of 1872.	...	307,628	...	307,637
District Fishery Boards	...	...	...	10,490
County Rates (including Roads, but excluding Police)			124,261	488,536
Parish Rates other than Poor Relief and Education	...	...	...	28,048
Total	126,923	1,849,555	204,261	869,274

INDEX

Accounts, local taxation, 11.
Administrative counties, 67.
Agricultural Rates Act, 144, 210, 236.
Agricultural system, primitive, 112.
Alcoholic liquors, sale of, 146.
Ashley (Mr.), quoted, 142.
Attendance, compulsory, at shire courts, 61.
Austin (John), definitions of government by, 9, 22.
Authorities, governing, relation of, to the electorate, 27, 235.
Authorities, local, in England, 12-13.

Baths and washhouses, 155.
Benefit, common, 119, 120.
Benefit, doctrine of, 178-207.
Benefit, taxation according to, 154, 155, 157, 158-169, 189-191, 212, 216, 250-254.
Bentham (Jeremy), quoted, 134.
Billingsgate market, 174.
Birlaw courts, 115-116.
Boroughs, municipal, 4, 15, 25, 37, 39, 75-105, 123, 224, 238.
Boundaries of boroughs, 97.
Bread, supply of, 142-144.
Buildings, control over, by local authorities, 169, 250.
Burial grounds, 155, 160-162, 246-248.
By-laws, 115, 119.

Canterbury, city of, 81, 90, 93.
Capital, private, demands of, 148, 149, 150, 152.
Cathedral closes, 41.
Children (pauper), authority having charge of, 13.
City organization, 86.
Coal supply, 145.

Coke (Lord), quoted, 119.
Collectivism, 73.
Co-ownership, 121.
Cornwall, county of, 59.
Coroner, office of, 61.
Corporate action, 121.
Counties, 4, 15, 36, 37, 39, 42-74, 103.
County boroughs, 75, 103.
Crawford birlaw court, 116.
Cunningham (Professor), quoted, 127, 132.
Customary law, 24.

Damage by riot, liability for, 73, 238.
Danish burghs, 85.
Definitions, elements of local government, 32-33; functions of local government, 187-188; principles of local government, 222-223.
Detached areas, 40, 236.
Development, principle of, 28, 192-207.
Devon, county of, 59.
Dialects, 47.
Differential taxation, 189-191.
Districts, 18, 19, 232, 234.
Ditmarsh community, 122, 243-245.
Docks and harbours, 150, 151, 154, 175, 250.
Dover harbour, 150.

Ecclesiastical parish, 107, 125-126.
Economics, public, 176-177.
Education Act, 6.
Education, elementary, 159.
Electorate of local government and State government practically the same, 3, 22, 24, 27, 29, 224, 225.
Electric light, 165.
Elements of local government, 32-33.

Exeter, early position of, 16, 85.

Federal government in relation to local government, 2.
Fire insurance, municipal, 150, 166–169.
Firma burgi, 91.
Food supply, 143.
Franchises, the great, 41, 130–177.
Functions of local government, 7–8, 130.

Gas supply, 155, 165.
Gloucester, property belonging to the corporation, 94, 239; water supply, 151.
Gothenburg system, 146.
Green (Mrs.), *Town Life*, quoted, 25, 142, 143.

Harbours, decay of, 150.
Herefordshire, shire-moot of, 50–52; condition of in 1610, 183, 237.
House, source of municipal rights, 94, 240.
House refuse, removal of, 158–159.
Hundred, the, 40, 72–74.
Hungary, county government in, 42.
Hustings, 63.

Incorporation of boroughs, 78–82.
Incorporation of parishes, 113.

Joint-stock associations, economical position of, 139.
Justices of peace, 62.

Kent, shire-moot of, 52–57, 64, 237, 238.
Kinship by blood, survival of, 88.

Laisser-faire school of economics, 137.
Land-owning by municipalities, 92, 241.
Lauder, 93.
Leadenhall market, 170.
Light railways, 6, 249.
Lincolnshire, ancient divisions of, granted county government, 67.
Liverpool docks, 151.
Locality, definitions of, 15, 20, 21, 128, 193.

Local government defined, 1; its relationship to State government, 4, 9, 235; phases of its history, 17–18; in relation to Austin's definitions, 22.
Locomotion, services of, 162–164, 248–249.
London, city of, 16, 77, 80, 85, 90, 93, 94, 100, 101, 105, 123, 144, 150, 151, 166, 170, 171, 173, 174, 226, 227, 241–242.
London, county of, 34, 40, 41, 67, 68, 69, 100, 105, 124, 125–126, 184, 190, 191, 193–194, 196, 197, 198, 199, 202, 225, 233.
London government reforms, 11, 226–231; additional authorities suggested, 232.
Long Acre, London, suggested origin of, 241.
Lubbock (Sir John), quoted, 142.

Maine (Sir Henry), quoted, 43, 91, 115.
Maitland (Professor), quoted, 46, 60, 95, 233.
Man (Isle of), government, 49–50.
Manorial element in township, 112, 114, 117, 122.
Markets, 154, 170–174.
Middlesex, county of, 40, 63, 241.
Mill (John Stuart), quoted, 138.

Officers, county, 70.
Old age, ancient cruelty towards, 182–183.
Open air, assemblies held in, 49, 101.
Outlawry, by county court, 63, 237.

Parishes, 5, 15, 37, 39, 100, 106–129, 195.
Pawnbroking, 145, 245.
Penge, in relation to London, 68.
Police service, administration of, 200–202.
Police, metropolitan, 19, 201, 232–234, 254–260.
Pollock (Sir Frederick), quoted, 59, 113.
Poor-law system, 179–186, 202–207.

INDEX

Poor-law unions, 18.
Positive law in relation to local government, 24.
Pound, village, 115.
Preston, 93, 94.
Prisons, administration of, 199–200.
Private action and public services, 135, 146, 148.
Profit, in relation to local services, 153.
Property, in relation to the community, 128, 131, 132, 169, 207, 213–214, 221.
Punishments, ancient, 111.

Railways, 162.
Rank, degrees of, in local authorities, 38–39, 71, 75, 76, 100.
Registration counties, 68–69.
Remunerative services, 153, 215, 263–264.
Ridings of Yorkshire granted county government, 67.
Roman influences, 77, 83, 97, 127, 242.
Russian mir, 89, 237.

St. Albans, 84.
Salford, 93.
Sanctions of local government, 24–27.
Scotland, 45, 85, 183, 263–264.
Seal (common) of counties, 59.
Seebohm (Mr.), quoted, 43, 112.
Settlement, law of, 204–206.
Sharing of taxation, principle of, 210–211.
Sheriff of London, 242.
Shires, English, 44–48, 237.

Shires, small, not equivalent to counties, 44, 237.
Silchester, 84.
Skene (Mr.), quoted, 45.
Socialism, 137, 147.
Spain, local government in, 235.
Spelman (Sir Henry), quoted, 162.
State government, 2, 8, 22, 26, 30, 235.
Stow's *London* quoted, 241.
Stubbs (Bishop), quoted, 113, 118.

Taxation, 64, 154, 157, 208–222, 262.
Taxation according to benefit, 154, 155, 157, 158–169, 189–191, 212, 216.
Taxation direct, 154, 157, 169.
Taxation indirect, 154, 157, 170.
Taxation, imperial, allotted to localities, 235–236, 260–261.
Telephones, 155, 164.
Townships, 5, 107–113, 123, 243.
Tramways, 155, 163, 164.
Tribal influences, 43–47, 236–237.

Utility, general, doctrine of, 134, 157, 178–207.

Vestry, modern, in relation to ancient township, 118.

Water supply, 13, 131, 150, 154, 169, 245–246.
Westminster, Henry III. and, 242.
Whitsome birlaw court, 116.
Wiltshire boroughs, 88–89.
Wiltshire townships, 109–110.
Winchester, 93, 173.

Reflections and Comments

BY

EDWIN LAWRENCE GODKIN

Crown 8vo, 7s. 6d.

"Mr. Godkin's book forms an excellent example of the best periodical literature of his country and time."—*The Daily News.*

"Mr. Godkin always writes pleasantly and suggestively."—*The Times.*

A NEW AND IMPORTANT BOOK

BY

EDWIN LAWRENCE GODKIN

Problems of Modern Democracy

Crown 8vo, 7s. 6d.

"These admirable essays . . . his handling of the various points and questions is marked by real grip, whilst the ease and clearness of his style make even the more technical of his essays eminently easy reading."—*The Glasgow Herald.*

"He talks freely, and always sensibly and to the point, and very often with more than ordinary wisdom."—*The Times.*

"As an anti-political observer Mr. Godkin will influence the reading public who, independently of differences of opinion, will unite in thanking him for an eminently suggestive book."—*Manchester Guardian.*

"The book ranks with Mr. Lecky's recent volumes."—*National Review.*

The Preaching of Islam
By T. W. ARNOLD, B.A.   *With 2 Maps.   Demy 8vo, 12s.*

"This book was wanted. . . . There has been no English book on Mahometanism printed since the well-known Dictionary, that is so informing and suggestive as this of Mr. Arnold's."—*Manchester Guardian.*

The Popular Religion and Folk-lore of Northern India
By WILLIAM CROOKE
With numerous Full-page Plates.   2 Vols.   Demy 8vo, 21s. net.

"The book is in every respect an admirable one, full of insight and knowledge at first hand."—*Times.*

Some Observations of a Foster Parent
By JOHN CHARLES TARVER
Crown 8vo, 6s.

"If there were more schoolmasters of the class to which Mr. Tarver evidently belongs, schoolmasters would be held in greater honour by those who have suffered at their hands. His 'Observations of a Foster Parent' are excellent reading; we hope they will reach the British parent. He may be assured the book is never dull."—*Glasgow Herald.*

"A very excellent book on the education of the English boy. The book is one which all parents should diligently read."—*Daily Mail.*

A BOOK FOR DANTE STUDENTS
The Chronicle of Villani
TRANSLATED BY ROSE E. SELFE.   EDITED BY THE REV. P. H. WICKSTEED.
Crown 8vo, 6s.

"We welcome the book not only as a real help to students of Dante, but as revealing to all English readers the leading characteristics of one of the most fascinating and lifelike of mediæval chronicles. . . . Mr. Wicksteed's introduction is brief, sober, competent, and workmanlike."—*Manchester Guardian.*

"Perhaps no one book is so important to the student of Dante as the chronicle of his contemporary Villani."—*Athenæum.*

English Schools.   1546–1548
By A. F. LEACH, M.A., F.S.A.,
Late Fellow of All Souls', Oxford, Assistant Charity Commissioner.
Demy 8vo, 12s.

"A very remarkable contribution to the history of secondary education in England, not less novel in its conclusions than important in the documentary evidence adduced to sustain them."—*The Times.*

"One of those books that, as soon as they are written, are regarded by the student as indispensable."—*Spectator.*

The Invasion of India by Alexander the Great
NEW AND REVISED EDITION.   WITH NUMEROUS ILLUSTRATIONS
By J. W. McCRINDLE
Demy 8vo, cloth gilt, 10s. 6d. net.

The English Scholar's Library

16 Parts are now published, in Cloth Boards, £2 1s. Any part may be obtained separately.

		s.	d.
1. WILLIAM CAXTON. **Reynard the Fox**		1	6
2. JOHN KNOX. **The First Blast of the Trumpet**		1	6
3. CLEMENT ROBINSON and *others*. **A Handful of Pleasant Delights**		1	6
4. [SIMON FISH.] **A Supplication for the Beggars**		1	6
5. [*Rev.* JOHN UDALL.] **Diotrephes**		1	6
6. [?] **The Return from Parnassus**		1	6
7. THOMAS DECKER. **The Seven Deadly Sins of London**		1	6
8. EDWARD ARBER. **An Introductory Sketch to the "Martin Marprelate" Controversy, 1588-1590**		3	0
9. [*Rev.* JOHN UDALL.] **A Demonstration of Discipline**		1	6
10. RICHARD STANIHURST. **"Æneid I.-IV."** in English hexameters		3	0
11. **"The Epistle"**		1	6
12. ROBERT GREEN. **Menaphon**		1	6
13. GEORGE JOY. **An Apology to William Tyndale**		1	6
14. RICHARD BARNFIELD. **Poems**		3	0
15. *Bp.* THOMAS COOPER. **An Admonition to the People of England**		3	0
16. *Captain* JOHN SMITH. **Works.** 1120 pages. Six Facsimile Maps. 2 Vols.		12	6

English Reprints

No.		Text.		s.	d.
1.	**Milton**	*Areopagitica*	1644	1	0
2.	**Latimer**	*The Ploughers*	1549	1	0
3.	**Gosson**	*The School of Abuse*	1579	1	0
4.	**Sidney**	*An Apology for Poetry*	? 1580	1	0
5.	**E. Webbe**	*Travels*	1590	1	0
6.	**Selden**	*Table Talk*	1634-54	1	0
7.	**Ascham**	*Toxophilus*	1544	1	0
8.	**Addison**	*Criticism on* Paradise Lost	1711-12	1	0
9.	**Lyly**	*EUPHUES*	1579-80	4	0
10.	**Villiers**	*The Rehearsal*	1671	1	0
11.	**Gascoigne**	*The Steel Glass, etc.*	1576	1	0
12.	**Earle**	*Micro-cosmographie*	1628	1	0
13.	**Latimer**	*Seven Sermons before* EDWARD VI.	1549	1	6
14.	**More**	*Utopia*	1516-57	1	0
15.	**Puttenham**	*The Art of English Poesy*	1589	2	6
16.	**Howell**	*Instructions for Foreign Travel*	1642	1	0
17.	**Udall**	*Roister Doister*	1553-66	1	0
18.	**Monk of Eves**	*The Revelation, etc.*	1180-1410	1	0
19.	**James I.**	*A Counterblast to Tobacco, etc.*	1604	1	0
20.	**Naunton**	*Fragmenta Regalia*	1653	1	0
21.	**Watson**	*Poems*	1582-93	1	6
22.	**Habington**	*CASTARA*	1640	1	0
23.	**Ascham**	*The Schoolmaster*	1570	1	0
24.	**Tottel's**	*Miscellany* [Songs and Sonnets]	1557	2	6
25.	**Lever**	*Sermons*	1550	1	0
26.	**W. Webbe**	*A Discourse of English Poetry*	1586	1	0
27.	**Lord Bacon**	*A Harmony of the Essays*	1597-1626	5	0
28.	**Roy, etc.**	*Read me, and be not wroth!*	1528	1	6
29.	**Raleigh, etc.**	*Last Fight of the " Revenge"*	1591	1	0
30.	**Googe**	*Eglogues, Epitaphs, and Sonnets*	1563	1	0

Boswell's Life of Johnson

Edited by AUGUSTINE BIRRELL.

WITH FRONTISPIECES BY ALEX ANSTED, A REPRODUCTION OF SIR JOSHUA REYNOLDS' PORTRAIT.

Six Volumes. Foolscap 8vo. Cloth, paper label, or gilt extra, 2s. net per Volume. Also half morocco, 3s. net per Volume. Sold in Sets only.

"Far and away the best Boswell, I should say, for the ordinary book-lover now on the market."—*Illustrated London News.*

". . . We have good reason to be thankful for an edition of a very useful and attractive kind."—*Spectator.*

"The volumes, which are light, and so well bound that they open easily anywhere, are exceedingly pleasant to handle and read."—*St. James's Budget.*

"This undertaking of the publishers ought to be certain of success."—*The Bookseller.*

"Read him at once if you have hitherto refrained from that exhilarating and most varied entertainment; or, have you read him?—then read him again."—*The Speaker.*

"Constable's edition will long remain the best both for the general reader and the scholar."—*Review of Reviews.*

In 48 Volumes

CONSTABLE'S REPRINT
OF
The Waverley Novels

THE FAVOURITE EDITION OF
SIR WALTER SCOTT.

With all the original Plates and Vignettes (Re-engraved). In 48 Vols.

Foolscap 8vo. Cloth, paper label title, 1s. 6d. net per Volume, or £3 12s. the Set. Also cloth gilt, gilt top, 2s. net per Volume, or £4 16s. the Set; and half leather gilt, 2s. 6d. net per Volume, or £6 the Set.

"A delightful reprint. The price is lower than that of many inferior editions."—*Athenæum.*

"The excellence of the print, and the convenient size of the volumes, and the association of this edition with Sir Walter Scott himself, should combine with so moderate a price to secure for this reprint a popularity as great as that which the original editions long and fully enjoyed with former generations of readers."—*The Times.*

"This is one of the most charming editions of the Waverley Novels that we know, as well as one of the cheapest in the market."—*Glasgow Herald.*

"Very attractive reprints."—*The Speaker.*

". . . Messrs. Constable & Co. have done good service to the reading world in reprinting them."—*Daily Chronicle.*

"The set presents a magnificent appearance on the bookshelf."—*Black and White.*

ARCHIBALD CONSTABLE & CO
2 WHITEHALL GARDENS WESTMINSTER

www.ingramcontent.com/pod-product-compliance
Lightning Source LLC
Chambersburg PA
CBHW032100220426
43664CB00008B/1082